Trust Management in the Internet of Vehicles

The Internet of Vehicles (IoV) is referred to as an efficient and inevitable convergence of the Internet of Things, intelligent transportation systems, edge / fog and cloud computing, and big data, all of which could be intelligently harvested for the cooperative vehicular safety and non-safety applications as well as cooperative mobility management. A secure and low-latency communication is, therefore, indispensable to meet the stringent performance requirements of the safety-critical vehicular applications.

Whilst the challenges surrounding low latency are being addressed by the researchers in both academia and industry, it is the *security* of an IoV network which is of paramount importance, as a *single* malicious message is perfectly capable enough of jeopardizing the entire networking infrastructure and can prove fatal for the vehicular passengers and the vulnerable pedestrians.

This book thus investigates the promising notion of trust in a bid to strengthen the resilience of the IoV networks. It not only introduces trust categorically in the context of an IoV network, i.e., in terms of its fundamentals and salient characteristics, but further envisages state-of-the-art trust models and intelligent trust threshold mechanisms for segregating both malicious and non-malicious vehicles. Furthermore, open research challenges and recommendations for addressing the same are discussed in the same too.

Adnan Mahmood possesses a PhD in Computer Science and is a Lecturer in Computing – IoT and Networking at the School of Computing, Macquarie University, Sydney, Australia. Before moving to Macquarie University, Adnan spent a considerable number of years in both the academic and research settings of the Republic of Ireland, Malaysia, Pakistan, and the People's Republic of China. His research interests include, but are not limited to, the Internet of Things (primarily, the Internet of Vehicles), Trust Management, Software-Defined Networking, and the Next Generation Heterogeneous Wireless Networks.

Quan Z. (Michael) Sheng is a full Professor and Head of the School of Computing at Macquarie University, Sydney, Australia. Michael holds a PhD in Computer Science from the University of New South Wales (UNSW), Australia. His research interests include Service Computing, Distributed Computing, Internet Technologies, and the Internet of Things. He is a recipient of the AMiner Most Influential Scholar Award on IoT (2019), ARC Future Fellowship (2014), Chris Wallace Award for Outstanding Research Contribution (2012), and the Microsoft Fellowship (2003). Michael is ranked by Microsoft Academic as one of the Most Impactful Authors in Services Computing (i.e., top five all time).

Wei Emma Zhang is a Lecturer in the School of Computer Science, the University of Adelaide, Australia and a Researcher in the promising paradigms of Information Retrieval, Natural Language Processing, and Text Mining. Wei obtained her PhD from the University of Adelaide and spent half a year in IBM Research, Australia as a full-time Intern. She further spent two and a half years at Macquarie University, Sydney as a Postdoctoral Researcher before joining the University of Adelaide.

Sira Yongchareon is currently an Associate Professor in the Department of Computer Science and Software Engineering at Auckland University of Technology, New Zealand. He received his PhD and MIT degrees from the Swinburne University, Melbourne, Australia. His research interest is in Ubiquitous / Pervasive Computing, including AI / Machine Learning and Data Management for the Internet of Things, Ambient Intelligence, Human Activity Recognition, Wireless Sensing, and Mobile / Edge Computing in Intelligent Environments.

Trust Management in the Internet of Vehicles

Adnan Mahmood, Michael Sheng,
Wei Emma Zhang and Sira Yongchareon

CRC Press
Taylor & Francis Group
Boca Raton London New York

CRC Press is an imprint of the
Taylor & Francis Group, an **informa** business

A CHAPMAN & HALL BOOK

First edition published 2024
by CRC Press
2385 NW Executive Center Drive, Suite 320, Boca Raton FL 33431

and by CRC Press
4 Park Square, Milton Park, Abingdon, Oxon, OX14 4RN

CRC Press is an imprint of Taylor & Francis Group, LLC

ISBN: 978-1-032-42950-2 (hbk)
ISBN: 978-1-032-42948-9 (pbk)
ISBN: 978-1-003-36503-7 (ebk)

DOI: 10.1201/9781003365037

Typeset in CMR10 font
by KnowledgeWorks Global Ltd.

Publisher's note: This book has been prepared from camera-ready copy provided by the authors.

To 'ones' in continuous pursuit of knowledge.

Authors

Contents

Preface

Over the past few decades, the considerable promising advancements in the telecommunications and automotive sectors have empowered drivers with highly innovative communication and sensing capabilities, in turn paving the way for the next-generation connected and autonomous vehicles. Today, vehicles possess the potential to communicate wirelessly with other vehicles and vulnerable pedestrians in their immediate vicinity in order to share timely safety-critical information (alerts) primarily for the purposes of collision mitigation. Furthermore, vehicles can seamlessly liaise with the traffic management entities via their supporting network infrastructure to become aware of any potential hazards on the roads and for guidance pertinent to their current and anticipated speeds and the traveling course to ensure more efficient traffic flows. This unprecedented evolution has thus led to the promising paradigm of the Internet of Vehicles (IoV) which is generally referred to as an intelligent and inevitable convergence of the Internet of Things, intelligent transportation systems, edge and/or fog and cloud computing, and big data that could be intelligently harvested for the cooperative vehicular safety (and non-safety) applications as well as cooperative mobility management. A secure and low-latency communication is, therefore, indispensable in order to meet the stringent performance requirements of safety-critical vehicular applications.

Whilst the challenges surrounding low latency are being addressed by the researchers in both academia and industry, i.e., primarily by developing state-of-the-art radio access technologies (RATs), and intelligent mechanisms for a heterogeneous amalgamation of several existing and new RATs together with their flexible deployment via a highly agile networking infrastructure, it is the *security* of an IoV network which is of paramount importance. It is indispensable to mention here that a *single* malicious message is usually capable enough of jeopardizing the entire networking infrastructure and can prove fatal for both the vehicular passengers and the vulnerable pedestrians.

Over the years, a considerable number of security techniques have been envisaged within the research literature for vehicular networking environments and which have fundamentally relied on the conventional cryptographic-based solutions employing both public key infrastructure and certificates. Nevertheless, it is pertinent to highlight here that: the conventional cryptographic-based solutions are not optimal for IoV networks as vehicles are highly dynamic in nature and are distributed throughout the network; the availability of a networking infrastructure cannot be guaranteed at all times; and cryptographic-based solutions are themselves susceptible to a poor key hygiene, compromised trust authorities, and insider attacks which are insidious and, therefore, capable of causing catastrophic damage.

Accordingly, this book employs the emerging yet promising notion of *trust* as an alternative for ensuring security within IoV networks. Trust itself is a derived quantity and is thus assigned to each vehicle in accordance with its behavior. It is contemplated as the currency of interaction between a trustor and a trustee. Nevertheless, weighing these vehicular interactions (often referred to as the *trust segments*) is indispensable in a bid to enhance the overall accuracy of a trust model and should be ascertained by taking into conformance the prior knowledge and context possessed by the corresponding one-hop neighboring vehicles, i.e., trustors, of a targeted vehicle, i.e., trustee. This book, therefore, envisages a distributed trust management system which ascertains the trust for all the reputation segments within an IoV network and further determines their respective weights by taking into account the salient characteristics (i.e., quality attributes) of familiarity, similarity, and timeliness. An intelligent trust threshold mechanism has also been envisaged which is capable of identifying and evicting misbehaving vehicles from an IoV network in an accurate manner. The performance of the envisaged IoV-based trust model has been investigated in terms of optimizing the misbehavior detection and its resilience to attacks. The experimental results depict that the envisaged IoV-based trust model outperforms other similar state-of-the-art trust models to a considerable extent in terms of optimizing the misbehavior detection and its resilience to attacks.

This book, furthermore, envisages a scalable hybrid trust-based model which introduces a composite metric encompassing the weighted amalgamation of a vehicle's computed trust score and its corresponding available resources to guarantee that the stringent performance requirements of the safety-critical vehicular applications could be met. Also, a Hungarian algorithm-based role assignment scheme has been envisaged for the selection of an optimal cluster head, proxy cluster head, and followers amongst the members of a vehicular cluster in an attempt to maximize its overall efficacy. The notion of an adaptive threshold has been proposed too in order to identify and subsequently eliminate the smart malicious vehicles from an IoV network in a timely manner, i.e., as soon as they start exhibiting an adverse behavior, to guarantee that the network is not manipulated for any malicious gains. The performance analysis demonstrates the efficaciousness of the envisaged scheme.

Adnan Mahmood
Quan Z. Sheng
Wei Emma Zhang
Sira Yongchareon

Authors

Adnan Mahmood possesses a PhD in Computer Science and is a Lecturer in Computing – IoT and Networking at the School of Computing, Macquarie University, Sydney, Australia. Before moving to Macquarie University, Adnan spent a considerable number of years in both academic and research settings of the Republic of Ireland, Malaysia, Pakistan, and the People's Republic of China. His research interests include, but are not limited to, the Internet of Things (primarily, the Internet of Vehicles), Trust Management, Software-Defined Networking, and the Next Generation Heterogeneous Wireless Networks. Adnan has 50+ publications as refereed book chapters, journal articles, and conference papers with a number of them published in prestigious venues, including but not limited to, ACM Computing Surveys, IEEE Transactions on Intelligent Transportation Systems, IEEE Transactions on Network and Service Management, ACM Transactions on Sensor Networks, ACM Transactions on Cyber-Physical Systems, and Nature's Scientific Reports. Adnan, besides, serves on the Technical Program Committees of a number of reputed international conferences. He is a member of the IEEE, IET, and the ACM.

Quan Z. (Michael) Sheng is a full Professor and Head of the School of Computing at Macquarie University, Sydney, Australia. His research interests include Service Computing, Distributed Computing, Internet Technologies, and the Internet of Things. Michael holds a PhD in Computer Science from the University of New South Wales (UNSW), Australia. He is the recipient of the AMiner Most Influential Scholar Award on IoT (2019), ARC Future Fellowship (2014), Chris Wallace Award for Outstanding Research Contribution (2012), and Microsoft Fellowship (2003). Michael is ranked by Microsoft Academic as one of the Most Impactful Author in Services Computing (i.e., top five all time). He is the Vice Chair of the Executive Committee of the IEEE Technical Community on Services Computing (IEEE TCSVC), the Associate Director (Smart Technologies) of Macquarie University Smart Green Cities Research Centre, and a member of the ACS (Australian Computer Society) Technical Advisory Board on IoT.

Wei Emma Zhang is a Lecturer in the School of Computer Science, the University of Adelaide, Australia and a Researcher in the promising paradigms of Information Retrieval, Natural Language Processing, and Text Mining. Wei obtained her PhD from the University of Adelaide and spent half a year in IBM Research, Australia as a full-time Intern. She further spent two and a half years in Macquarie University, Sydney as a Postdoctoral Researcher before joining the University of Adelaide. Wei has close to 100 publications in the form of edited books and proceedings, refereed book chapters, and refereed technical papers in journals and conferences. She published a monograph in Springer in August 2018 on Managing Data and Knowledge Bases. Her papers have been published in prestigious journals in Computer Science, including but not limited to, the ACM Transactions on Internet Technology, World Wide Web Journal, Communications of the ACM, ACM Transactions on Intelligent Systems and Technology, IEEE Transactions on Services Computing, and IEEE Transactions on Big Data. Wei's research has further appeared in top-tier international conferences including the Web Conference, International Conference on Extending Database Technology, International Conference on Information and Knowledge Management, International Conference on Service Oriented Computing, and International Conference on Web Services.

Sira Yongchareon is an Associate Professor in the Department of Computer Science and Software Engineering at the Auckland University of Technology, New Zealand. He received his PhD and MIT degrees from Swinburne University, Melbourne, Australia in 2012 and 2008, respectively. Before that, he worked as a Software Engineer for seven years subsequent to receiving his B.Eng in Computer Engineering from King Mongkut Institute of Technology Lardkrabang, Bangkok, Thailand in 1999. His research interest is in Ubiquitous / Pervasive Computing, including AI / Machine Learning and Data Management for the Internet of Things, Ambient Intelligence, Human Activity Recognition, Wireless Sensing, and Mobile / Edge Computing in Intelligent Environments. He has publications in numerous reputable journals and conferences, such as IEEE TSC, IEEE IoT, ACM CSUR, FGCS, KBS, ESWA, Information Systems, ACM TMIS, Computing, IEEE Sensors, Computer in Industry, WWWJ, IEEE TrustCom, IEEE Service Computing, Web Information Systems Engineering, and Business Process Management. He has served on the program committees of a number of international conferences and was invited as a reviewer of high-quality journals, including IEEE IoT, IEEE TSMC, ACM TSC, ACM TMIS, JSS, WWWJ, and SPE. Sira is a senior member of IEEE and ACM.

List of Figures

List of Tables

1

Introduction

Over the past few decades, the promising notion of Vehicular Ad hoc Networks (VANETs) has been thoroughly studied and well-researched in both academia and industry. Nevertheless, the emerging yet promising paradigms of the cloud computing, fog and edge computing, Software Defined Networks (SDN), and network functions virtualization have not only completely revolutionized the wireless networking industry but have further triggered considerable innovative advancements for the transportation sector too [1, 2, 3, 4, 5]. This is coupled with other recent significant technological advances pertinent to the evolution of connected and autonomous vehicles and a pervasive usage of the numerous state-of-the-art sensory devices installed onboard vehicles which facilitate in a diverse range of cooperative vehicular safety applications such as forward collision warnings, emergency vehicular assistance, (vulnerable) pedestrian collision mitigation, blind intersection warnings, and hazardous location warnings, amongst many others. The said safety applications are not only extremely critical in nature but further require a low-latency supporting infrastructure with a maximum permissible tolerable delay ranging in-between 3 and 10 ms [6, 7].

Furthermore, modern-day connected vehicles are equipped with on average 100 sensors onboard and this number is anticipated to increase up to 200 in a matter of no time [3, 8]. These sensors are not only responsible for generating a bulk amount of data but also play an indispensable role in creating and sharing of ambient intelligence for vehicular cooperative communication. The emerging paradigm of ambient intelligence is primarily reliant on considerable research advances in sensors and sensor networks, context-aware computing, ubiquitous and pervasive computing, and artificial intelligence, and empowers any vehicle embedded with a network of intelligent devices to sense its immediate environment, anticipate, and adapt accordingly [9]. Moreover, as per an estimate of Intel Corporation [10], an averagely-driven connected vehicle (i.e., a personal vehicle employed for day-to-day routine purposes and not for commercial operations) in the near future would generate approximately 4,000 GB (4 TB) of data for every hour of its driving. Both Dell Technologies and the Automotive Edge Computing Consortium have lately put this estimate to be around 5.17 TB per hour of a vehicle's driving [11]. This estimate could also be compared with the data consumption of an average Internet user which has been anticipated to reach up to 1.66 GB per day by the end of year 2024[1][12].

The questions, therefore, arise as (a) how to tackle such a massive flood of data so that the meaningful information could be accumulated, processed, and utilized for the above-referred vehicular safety applications; (b) which particular Radio Access Technologies (RATs) would be able to facilitate the transmission of such a meaningful information with extremely higher data rates and lower end-to-end delay; (c) where this all processing, i.e., compute and storage, needs to be tackled as sending of the data back to the remote back-end servers would not only require an excessive bandwidth but may also result in excessive load on the backhaul, thereby increasing the network management overhead and compromising the service-level objectives of diverse vehicular safety applications, and above all, (d) how to fully ensure the resilience of the network so that the processed data (meaningful information) is securely transmitted to its intended destination without being altered, forged, or dropped by any malicious intruder. Each of this question, in its own essence, is a gigantic challenge and justice cannot be done to all of them within a single book.

It is also pertinent to mention here that a considerable amount of research has already been and is currently being carried out in tackling the issues pertinent to big data's accumulation, transmission, storage, and computing in a vehicular networking context. Similarly, researchers in academia and industry have been off lately devising state-of-the-art RATs, and intelligent mechanisms for a heterogeneous amalgamation of the existing and new RATs together with their flexible deployment via a highly agile networking infrastructure, in order to guarantee a rapid network innovation for mitigating potential chances of network fragmentation and an inefficient resource utilization. Nevertheless, it is, in fact, the *security* of a vehicular network which is of the utmost importance; i.e., if a vehicular network is not secure, it would result in dire repercussions for the entire network and particularly for the occupants of the vehicles and the vulnerable pedestrians.

1.1   State of the Art in Intelligent Transportation Systems

Vehicular networking is one of the key technologies that caters to the realization of a variety of the aforementioned safety-critical vehicular applications

---

[1]There is a lot of ongoing hype at this stage in the automotive industry pertinent to the data generation of autonomous vehicles. The real volume would undoubtedly vary depending on a car's activity and a precise estimate of the same could not be ascertained until the technology reaches its maturity and is fully rolled out. Nevertheless, one thing remains obvious; i.e., it would undoubtedly be a flood of data.

[13, 14, 15, 16]. These safety applications allow for a collection and dissemination of useful contextual information between the vehicles (Vehicle-to-Vehicle (V2V) communication), between the vehicles and the supporting infrastructure (Vehicle-to-Infrastructure (V2I) communication), between the vehicles and the supporting network (Vehicle-to-Network (V2N) communication), and between the vehicles and the vulnerable pedestrians (Vehicle-to-Pedestrian (V2P) communication), thereby strengthening the foundation for the emerging yet promising paradigm of Vehicle-to-Everything (V2X) communication. Therefore, a highly secure and low-latency communication between the vehicles, and amongst the vehicles and the supporting infrastructure and the network, is quite indispensable to the successful implementation of such applications [15, 16]. V2X communication makes vehicles an integral constituent of the Internet of Things (IoT) landscape and, accordingly, the emerging yet promising paradigm of the Internet of Vehicles (IoV) has recently started taking its place within the research literature.

A brief glimpse of the research literature reveals numerous research studies that surveyed the potential challenges and limitations for devising an efficacious ITS [17]. Some of these research studies (a) presented a comprehensive overview of LTE-based V2X standardization activities, and further addressed two key technical challenges, i.e., dense vehicular environments and higher mobilities, in fulfilling the V2X service requirements along with numerous technical design considerations [18]; (b) outlined a systematic investigation of the existing vehicular communication systems in terms of their potential benefits, limitations (congestion owing to a large network size and heavy traffic load, intermittent connections due to high mobility and sparse roadside units' deployment, backhaul delay, and delays in ensuring security of the vehicular network via legitimization of messages), diverse vehicular applications and system requirements, and further envisaged a layered-5G vehicular networking architecture encompassing numerous diverse RATs, vehicles, and roadside units' space [19]; and (c) studied the automotive sensing technologies employed for active safety measures [20] and opined 5G mmWave communication as the only feasible option for the high bandwidth connected vehicles [8].

Similarly, some other ITS-related research studies (a) surveyed the state-of-the-art vehicular localization techniques (and their performance and applicability for the autonomous vehicles) which, in particular, focused on the sensor-based technologies for ascertaining the position of vehicles on a specified coordinate system and their combination with the cooperative techniques (V2V and V2I communication via numerous wireless communication technologies) in order to enhance the locational accuracy and reliability [21]; (b) investigated the relationship between big data and IoV in a vehicular context and focused on how IoV facilitates in the big data acquisition, ensures a seamless ubiquitous big data transmission (with its challenges being harsh wireless channel conditions, spectrum resource shortage, high mobility of vehicles, dynamic vehicle density, and absence of global coordination), and enhances the storage and computing abilities for the same [22]; and (c) deliberated on a big data-enabled IoV and evaluated how big data mining and machine learning mechanisms could bring considerable advantages for the IoV development in certain aspects including, but not limited to, the network characterizations, intelligent protocol design, and performance evaluation [22, 23].

Security is also one of the indispensable characteristics in designing a highly efficient and cooperative ITS and, therefore, demands a careful deliberation. Some of the security-related research studies in ITS have presented a self-contained and systematic survey encompassing security, privacy, and trust-related challenges pertaining to VANETs (a need to fully secure both the V2V and V2I channels; the need for a privacy protection mechanism as a supplementary to anonymous authentication schemes to mitigate the threat transpiring as a result of a tracking attack; and how a vehicle could trust other vehicles and their corresponding messages?), and highlighted a number of anonymous authentication mechanisms, location privacy protection mechanisms, and trust management models along with their efficaciousness [24]. Moreover, state-of-the-art VANET security architectures, frameworks, security standards and protocols, classification of several critical vehicular security attacks along with their probable solutions, and challenges (size of the network, high mobility, dynamic network topology, keys distribution, and forwarding algorithms) which act as the bottlenecks in the evolution of secure ITS architectures, together with future research directions, have been discussed [25].

A comprehensive survey pertinent to the state-of-the-art solutions concerning security and privacy in V2X communication has been presented in [26], wherein both cryptographic-based schemes; i.e., batch and non-batch verification, and trust-based schemes have been discussed together with an illustration on both privacy preservation and location preservation schemes. Several research challenges including, but not limited to, the need for an efficient re-batching algorithm for the batch verification schemes primarily under an ultra-dense scenario, efficient revocation mechanisms in order to speed up the revocation process of both malicious vehicles and their messages, integrating cryptography and trust so as to formulate a single robust and scalable vehicular communication system to tackle both internal and external attacks, effective and efficient intrusion detection mechanisms for identifying and tracing inside attackers, and a general simulation platform encompassing a number of vehicular network scenarios and V2X uses cases to facilitate researchers to carry out comprehensive evaluations and comparisons have been discussed.

It is also pertinent to highlight that the research focus of the ITS community has recently shifted from the conventional cryptographic-based security solutions, i.e., the ones based on certificates and public key infrastructures, to trust management schemes [13, 27]. Although a number of research studies have envisaged trust models in a vehicular networking context, wherein a trustor evaluates the trust of a trustee by primarily ascertaining both the direct trust and the indirect trust (recommendations), nevertheless,

challenges including, but not limited to, trust bootstrapping, trust aggregation, decay/lifetime of a trust value, lack of incentive mechanisms for stimulating the participation of selfish vehicles in the trust evaluation process,
and ephemeral communications owing to the unpredictable interconnection
time among different vehicles, still need considerable attention. Furthermore,
the need for reputation management mechanisms to strategically motivate
the vehicles in order to maintain a good reputation in case of possessing limited network resources, an end-to-end trust management mechanism for the
seamless integration of VANETs with enabling technologies since trust management is tackled differently in different environments, and a context-aware
trust management scheme for ensuring an adaptive trust management mechanism to invoke the respective trust evaluation strategy in accordance with
the particular environment, requires further deliberation [1].

Moreover, research studies evaluating the technical feasibilities and performance analyses of wireless networking technologies supporting numerous
diverse vehicular applications have been conducted. Some of these studies (a)
evaluated performance of diverse heterogeneous vehicular networks (encompassing DSRC, LTE, and Wi Fi) for both V2V and V2I communication and
further envisaged an application layer handoff scheme that not only guaranteed an optimal utilization of the available wireless technologies but further
ensured minimizing of corresponding backhaul communication requirements
[28]; (b) proposed a signaling game-based scheme in order to guarantee an
always best connected service for vehicles traversing in a geographical region equipped with heterogeneous wireless networks [29]; and (c) envisaged
a multi-tier heterogeneous adaptive vehicular networking architecture integrating LTE and DSRC technologies in order to warrant both reliability and
low-latency for safety-critical message dissemination within a vehicular networking environment by balancing the network traffic through offloading the
packet forwarding from the cellular networks [30]. Even though the interwork-
ing of multiple networking technologies facilitate in reaping the advantages
of one technology while reasonably offsetting the disadvantages of the other,
nevertheless, when and how to opt for an appropriate technology for each of
the communication link and ensuring a seamless handoff among the different technologies is a challenging chore in its own essence [31]. This becomes
extremely indispensable since vehicles dynamically traverse both in and out
of the communication ranges of the other vehicles and supporting networking
infrastructure, thus resulting in frequent changes in the network topology and
frequently disconnected V2V and V2I communication links. Security is yet
another associated challenge at the time of the handover since the security
key needs to be changed for different connections.

As of late, the emerging yet promising paradigm of SDN has been exploited for VANETs. Although the said paradigm is in its infancy, nonethe-
less, some of the research studies in this particular paradigm (a) suggested
a scalable and responsive SDN-enabled vehicular networking architecture,
facilitated with mobile edge computing, to minimize the data transmission

time and for improving the overall quality-of-experience of the vehicular users for a diverse range of latency-sensitive applications [32]; (b) envisaged a hierarchical SDN-based architecture for vehicular networks, together with a communication protocol, in order to address the lack of connection/coordination from a centralized SDN controller [33]; and (c) presented an architecture supporting the cohesion of SDN and named data networking to fetch the requisite content in the vehicular networks, wherein a name is assigned to the content (instead of the device, i.e., vehicle or infrastructure) and a pull-based communication approach is then used to retrieve the requisite content, as and when desired [34]. Nevertheless, several architectural design challenges need to be addressed for its full scale implementation including, but not limited to, ensuring of a seamless, ubiquitous, and undifferentiated network connectivity and a reliable and cost-efficient heterogeneous communication via multi hop routing, broadcast storm mitigation via appropriate network slicing, tackling the highly dynamic and distributed behavior of vehicles (as this is the key root cause of all the vehicular networking challenges), ensuring security by mitigating the possibility of a malicious vehicle either manipulating the SDN controller or spoofing itself as a fake SDN controller; i.e., identity spoofing, and introducing an optimal mobility-aware edge caching policy to minimize the average delay of a vehicle (or a vehicular user's) request [35].

An abridged (self-contained) summary of research challenges surrounding next-generation ITS architectures is depicted in Figure 1.1. Whilst a number of research challenges have been depicted herein, nevertheless, this book would categorically focus on addressing the *security aspects* within a vehicular networking context by employing the notion of *trust management*.

1.2   Aims and Significance of the Book

Security is undoubtedly the most indispensable concern within a vehicular networking environment. This becomes even more of an issue with our evergrowing desire to make vehicles more and more intelligent and seamlessly connected to the Internet. This desire has overtime led to the evolution of VANETs into IoV, wherein vehicles employ V2V communication in a bid to exchange safety-critical and non-safety, i.e., infotainment, messages with one another, V2I and V2N communication for communicating with the supporting roadside infrastructure, i.e., traffic lights and the parking spaces, and with the backbone network (data centers), respectively, and V2P communication to interact with the smartphone-toting vulnerable pedestrians. All of this falls under the umbrella of V2X communication, wherein information propagates via a high-bandwidth, low-latent communication link to ensure highly secure and intelligent traffic flows. All of this is also integral to the futuristic 5G

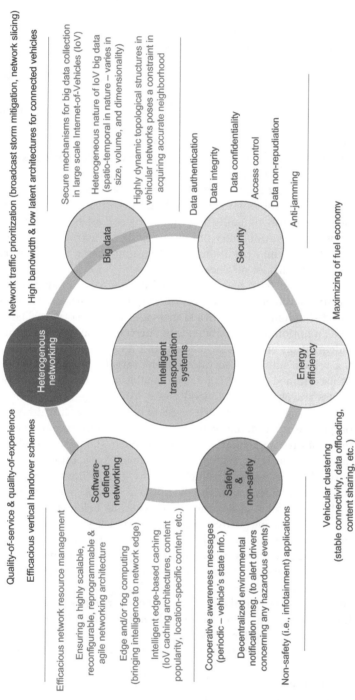

FIGURE 1.1

Research challenges surrounding next-generation ITS architectures.

networks and is indispensable for the technological evolution of connected and autonomous vehicles and smart cities [36, 37].

However, safety-critical communication within an IoV context could not be realized until a network is completely secure since the dissemination of even a *single* malicious message not only possesses the potential of jeopardizing the entire network but could further transpire in a number of fatalities on the road. It is, therefore, of the utmost importance that these malicious entities, and their corresponding messages, be identified and subsequently eliminated in an instant manner from an IoV network before they are able to manipulate the entire network for their own malicious gains. Over the years, a considerable number of security techniques have been envisaged for vehicular networks primarily relying on the conventional cryptographic-based solutions which utilize public key infrastructure and certificates [27]. Nevertheless, it is pertinent to highlight that the cryptographic-based solutions are not optimal for IoV networks since vehicles are highly dynamic in nature and are distributed throughout the entire network, the availability of a networking infrastructure cannot be guaranteed at all times, and traditional cryptographic-based solutions are themselves vulnerable to insider attacks.

Therefore, the notion of *trust* has been lately introduced as an alternative for ensuring security in vehicular networks. In trust-based schemes, vehicles communicate and disseminate safety-critical messages with the other vehicles based on trust, i.e., a notion of the confidence of one vehicle on the other, and which is an amalgamation of both direct trust and an indirect trust. Direct trust is, in fact, a vehicle's direct observation of the targeted vehicle, whereas indirect trust is ascertained by seeking recommendations from the one-hop neighboring vehicles traversing in the vicinity of a targeted vehicle. Furthermore, it is pertinent to highlight that each one-hop neighbor that furnishes its recommendation possesses a different context (i.e., both conditions and capabilities) and, hence, its recommendation (trust) segment should be weighted accordingly. Therefore, the trust segments determined for a targeted vehicle via all of its one-hop neighboring vehicles at any given time instance are appropriately aggregated to ascertain the overall trust of a targeted vehicle. Moreover, once the trust value of a targeted vehicle falls below a particular threshold, i.e., the trustworthiness threshold, the said vehicle should be labeled as a misbehaving one and is subsequently removed from an IoV network.

Such direct and indirect observations are not only realistic in nature but could be also put into practice primarily owing to a rapid evolution and an accelerated deployment of connected vehicles, i.e., duly embedded with state-of-the-art sensing technologies, in the context of the smart cities. The essence here is to carefully ascertain the behavior of each individual vehicle in an IoV network since a misbehaving vehicle may act (a) maliciously by either partially or entirely dropping the messages received from a trustor (instead of relaying them onward), (b) in an intelligent dishonest mode via demonstrating malicious and non-malicious behavior to avoid identification, or (c) in a selfish mode (it only participates in the network when it best suits its own interests). Whilst there is always a possibility for incentivizing the selfish vehicles to participate in the network, it is, in fact, the malicious and intelligent dishonest vehicles that have the intent of not only bad-mouthing the trustworthy vehicles but for also inflicting severe harm to other entities within an IoV network. Hence, a vehicle intentionally dropping partial or entire messages in an IoV network for any particular duration of time should be identified and subsequently eliminated from an IoV network. This, therefore, facilitates in designing a highly intelligent vehicular networking environment by facilitating vehicles to exchange sensitive information with one another in a secure manner.

The book-at-hand primarily addresses two open key issues in order to guarantee a trusted IoV network which can facilitate in realizing a safe deployment of futuristic connected and autonomous vehicles. The specific research questions addressed by this book are as follows:

1. How to formulate an intelligent, scalable, and resilient state-of-the-art IoV-based trust computational model that is capable of ascertaining the trust score of a targeted vehicle, i.e., trustee, by taking into consideration both direct and indirect reputation segments (and their corresponding weights via relevant quality attributes), and further ensures a timely identification and subsequent elimination of misbehaving vehicles from an IoV network?

2. How to opt for a trusted and resource efficient cluster head amongst the members of a vehicular cluster in order to not only maximize a cluster's overall efficacy but to further ensure that the stringent performance requirements of the safety-critical vehicular applications could be fully met?

1.3 Contributions of the Book

This book delineates on the convergence of the promising notion of trust with the IoV in terms of not only its underlying rationale but also by highlighting the salient opportunities it offers for strengthening the security of an IoV network together with the challenges that should be intelligently addressed for realizing the deployment of the trusted IoV networks in the context of the smart cities.

It also envisages a state-of-the-art trust computational model for ascertaining the trust of a trustee, i.e., targeted vehicle, by taking into consideration all of its reputation segments within an IoV environment. Since the accuracy of each individual reputation segment is of the paramount significance, appropriate weights have been hence ascertained for all of the reputation segments via some quality attributes encompassing both the prior knowledge and the context possessed by the respective one-hop neighboring vehicles of any targeted vehicle. The performance of the IoV-based trust model is studied both in terms of optimizing the misbehavior detection and its resilience to attacks.

Moreover, once the aggregated trust has been ascertained for a trustee in an IoV network, an optimal threshold needs to be determined so as to identify the misbehaving vehicles, i.e., vehicles satisfying the said threshold should be considered as trustworthy ones, whereas, the ones falling beneath the said threshold should be regarded as untrustworthy ones. Therefore, an optimal threshold is of the essence since if it is set extremely high would, in turn, result in the elimination of the trustworthy vehicles. On the contrary, if an optimal threshold is too low, it would facilitate the misbehaving vehicles to keep on manipulating the entire network for their (personal) malicious gains. Accordingly, this book envisages an intelligent trust threshold mechanism that is capable of identifying and evicting misbehaving vehicles in an efficacious manner. The introduction of an inspection threshold, together with an allocation of additional time to vehicles being inspected under certain specific conditions, serve as an additional check in order to guarantee that only misbehaving vehicles are removed from an IoV network and vehicles which are in fact bad-mouthed by the misbehaving vehicles can be reintegrated into the network.

Furthermore, since connected vehicles are anticipated to traverse in the form of vehicular clusters, the role of a cluster head becomes of the essence as they are not only responsible for both intra- and inter-cluster communication, but for communicating the entire cluster's status to the network edge and the backhaul primarily as to mitigate the excessive network management overhead. Moreover, given the critical role of a cluster head in a cluster, there would be dire repercussions if a misbehaving vehicle gets elected as the cluster head. Therefore, it is indispensable to elect an appropriate vehicle as the cluster head from amongst the members of a cluster. Nevertheless, possessing of a highest trust score does not necessarily justifies a vehicle's eligibility as a cluster head. In fact, apart from being categorized as the trustworthy one, a vehicle that can guarantee the efficacy of the entire cluster should be considered as an optimal choice for the role of a cluster head. In this regard, this book further proposes a scalable hybrid trust model which introduces a composite metric (encompassing the weighted amalgamation of a vehicle's computed trust score and its corresponding available resources) and an optimal role assignment scheme as to ensure that the stringent performance requirements of the safety-critical vehicular applications could be fully met and the overall efficacy of any vehicular cluster within an IoV network could be maximized. Also, the notion of an adaptive threshold has been proposed in order to identify and subsequently eliminate the smart malicious vehicles from an IoV network in a timely manner, i.e., as soon as they start exhibiting an adverse behavior, to guarantee that the network is not manipulated for any malicious gains.

Bibliography

[1] Rasheed Hussain, Jooyoung Lee, and Sherali Zeadally. Trust in VANET: A Survey of Current Solutions and Future Research Opportunities. *IEEE Transactions on Intelligent Transportation Systems*, 22(5):2553–2571, 2021.

[2] Baofeng Ji, Xueru Zhang, Shahid Mumtaz, Congzheng Han, Chunguo Li, Hong Wen, and Dan Wang. Survey on the Internet of Vehicles: Network Architectures and Applications. *IEEE Communications Standards Magazine*, 4(1):34–41, 2020.

[3] Adnan Mahmood, Wei Zhang, and Quan Sheng. Software-Defined Heterogeneous Vehicular Networking: The Architectural Design and Open Challenges. *Future Internet*, 11(3):70, 2019.

[4] Kai Wang, Hao Yin, Wei Quan, and Geyong Min. Enabling Collaborative Edge Computing for Software Defined Vehicular Networks. *IEEE Network*, 32(5):112–117, 2018.

[5] Tasneem S. J. Darwish and Kamalrulnizam Abu Bakar. Fog Based Intelligent Transportation Big Data Analytics in The Internet of Vehicles Environment: Motivations, Architecture, Challenges, and Critical Issues. *IEEE Access*, 6:15679–15701, 2018.

[6] Haibo Zhou, Wenchao Xu, Jiacheng Chen, and Wei Wang. Evolutionary V2X Technologies Toward the Internet of Vehicles: Challenges and Opportunities. *Proceedings of the IEEE*, 108(2):308–323, 2020.

[7] 3GPP. Technical Specification Group Services and System Aspects: Enhancement of 3GP Support for V2X Scenarios (22.186 v16.2.0). Technical report, France, 2019.

[8] Junil Choi, Vutha Va, Nuria Gonzalez-Prelcic, Robert Daniels, Chandra R. Bhat, and Robert W. Heath. Millimeter-Wave Vehicular Communication to Support Massive Automotive Sensing. *IEEE Communications Magazine*, 54(12):160–167, 2016.

[9] Paulo Novais and Gabriel Villarrubia González. Challenges and Trends in Ambient Intelligence. *Journal of Ambient Intelligence and Humanized Computing*, 11(11):4405–4408, 2020.

[10] Just One Autonomous Car Will Use 4,000 GB of Data/Day. `https://www.networkworld.com`, note = Accessed: 2023-07-1.

[11] Rolling ZBs: Quantifying the Data Impact of Connected Cars. `https://www.datacenterfrontier.com/connected-cars/article/11429212/rolling-zettabytes-quantifying-the-data-impact-of-connected-cars`.

[12] Ericsson. Ericsson Mobility Report – November 2018. Technical report, Stockholm, Sweden, 2018.

[13] Aljawharah Alnasser, Hongjian Sun, and Jing Jiang. Recommendation-Based Trust Model for Vehicle-to-Everything (V2X). *IEEE Internet of Things Journal*, 7(1):440–450, 2020.

[14] Carlos Renato Storck and Fátima Duarte-Figueiredo. A Survey of 5G Technology Evolution, Standards, and Infrastructure Associated With Vehicle-to-Everything Communications by Internet of Vehicles. *IEEE Access*, 8:117593–117614, 2020.

[15] Monowar Hasan, Sibin Mohan, Takayuki Shimizu, and Hongsheng Lu. Securing Vehicle-to-Everything (V2X) Communication Platforms. *IEEE Transactions on Intelligent Vehicles*, 5(4):693–713, 2020.

[16] Gaurang Naik, Biplav Choudhury, and Jung-Min Park. IEEE 802.11bd & 5G NR V2X: Evolution of Radio Access Technologies for V2X Communications. *IEEE Access*, 7:70169–70184, 2019.

[17] Haijian Li, Guoqiang Zhao, Lingqiao Qin, Hanimaiti Aizeke, Xiaohua Zhao, and Yanfang Yang. A Survey of Safety Warnings Under Connected Vehicle Environments. *IEEE Transactions on Intelligent Transportation Systems*, 22(5):2572–2588, 2021.

[18] Hanbyul Seo, Ki-Dong Lee, Shinpei Yasukawa, Ying Peng, and Philippe Sartori. LTE Evolution for Vehicle-to-Everything Services. *IEEE Communications Magazine*, 54(6):22–28, 2016.

[19] Konstantinos Katsaros and Mehrdad Dianati. *A Conceptual 5G Vehicular Networking Architecture*, pages 595–623. Springer International Publishing, Cham, 2017.

[20] Kayhan Zrar Ghafoor, Linghe Kong, Sherali Zeadally, Ali Safaa Sadiq, Gregory Epiphaniou, Mohammad Hammoudeh, Ali Kashif Bashir, and Shahid Mumtaz. Millimeter-Wave Communication for Internet of Vehicles: Status, Challenges, and Perspectives. *IEEE Internet of Things Journal*, 7(9):8525–8546, 2020.

[21] Sampo Kuutti, Saber Fallah, Konstantinos Katsaros, Mehrdad Dianati, Francis Mccullough, and Alexandros Mouzakitis. A Survey of the State-of-the-Art Localization Techniques and Their Potentials for Autonomous Vehicle Applications. *IEEE Internet of Things Journal*, 5(2):829–846, 2018.

[22] Wenchao Xu, Haibo Zhou, Nan Cheng, Feng Lyu, Weisen Shi, Jiayin Chen, and Xuemin Shen. Internet of Vehicles in Big Data Era. *IEEE/CAA Journal of Automatica Sinica*, 5(1):19–35, 2018.

[23] Nan Cheng, Feng Lyu, Jiayin Chen, Wenchao Xu, Haibo Zhou, Shan Zhang, and Xuemin Shen. Big Data Driven Vehicular Networks. *IEEE Network*, 32(6):160–167, 2018.

[24] Zhaojun Lu, Gang Qu, and Zhenglin Liu. A Survey on Recent Advances in Vehicular Network Security, Trust, and Privacy. *IEEE Transactions on Intelligent Transportation Systems*, 20(2):760–776, 2019.

[25] Hamssa Hasrouny, Abed Ellatif Samhat, Carole Bassil, and Anis Laouiti. VANet Security Challenges and Solutions: A Survey. *Vehicular Communications*, 7:7–20, 2017.

[26] Jiaqi Huang, Dongfeng Fang, Yi Qian, and Rose Qingyang Hu. Recent Advances and Challenges in Security and Privacy for V2X Communications. *IEEE Open Journal of Vehicular Technology*, 1:244–266, 2020.

[27] Farhan Ahmad, Virginia N. L. Franqueira, and Asma Adnane. TEAM: A Trust Evaluation and Management Framework in Context-Enabled Vehicular Ad-Hoc Networks. *IEEE Access*, 6:28643–28660, 2018.

[28] Kakan Chandra Dey, Anjan Rayamajhi, Mashrur Chowdhury, Parth Bhavsar, and James Martin. Vehicle-to-Vehicle (V2V) and Vehicle-to-Infrastructure (V2I) Communication in a Heterogeneous Wireless Network – Performance Evaluation. *Transportation Research Part C: Emerging Technologies*, 68:168–184, 2016.

[29] Abdelfettah Mabrouk, Abdellatif Kobbane, Essaid Sabir, Jalel Ben-Othman, and Mohammed El Koutbi. Meeting Always-Best-Connected Paradigm in Heterogeneous Vehicular Networks: A Graph Theory and a Signaling Game Analysis. *Vehicular Communications*, 5:1–8, 2016.

[30] S. Ansari, T. Boutaleb, S. Sinanovic, C. Gamio, and I. Krikidis. MHAV: Multitier Heterogeneous Adaptive Vehicular Network with LTE and DSRC. *ICT Express*, 3(4):199–203, 2017. SI: Intelligent Transportation Communication Systems.

[31] Haixia Peng, Le Liang, Xuemin Shen, and Geoffrey Ye Li. Vehicular Communications: A Network Layer Perspective. *IEEE Transactions on Vehicular Technology*, 68(2):1064–1078, 2019.

[32] Jianqi Liu, Jiafu Wan, Bi Zeng, Qinruo Wang, Houbing Song, and Meikang Qiu. A Scalable and Quick-Response Software Defined Vehicular Network Assisted by Mobile Edge Computing. *IEEE Communications Magazine*, 55(7):94–100, 2017.

[33] Sergio Correia, Azzedine Boukerche, and Rodolfo I. Meneguette. An Architecture for Hierarchical Software-Defined Vehicular Networks. *IEEE Communications Magazine*, 55(7):80–86, 2017.

[34] Syed Hassan Ahmed, Safdar Hussain Bouk, Dongkyun Kim, Danda B. Rawat, and Houbing Song. Named Data Networking for Software Defined Vehicular Networks. *IEEE Communications Magazine*, 55(8):60–66, 2017.

[35] Othman S. Al-Heety, Zahriladha Zakaria, Mahamod Ismail, Mohammed Mudhafar Shakir, Sameer Alani, and Hussein Alsariera. A Comprehensive Survey: Benefits, Services, Recent Works, Challenges, Security, and Use Cases for SDN-VANET. *IEEE Access*, 8:91028–91047, 2020.

[36] Joshua E. Siegel, Dylan C. Erb, and Sanjay E. Sarma. A Survey of the Connected Vehicle Landscape—Architectures, Enabling Technologies, Applications, and Development Areas. *IEEE Transactions on Intelligent Transportation Systems*, 19(8):2391–2406, 2018.

[37] Rongxing Lu, Lan Zhang, Jianbing Ni, and Yuguang Fang. 5G Vehicle-to-Everything Services: Gearing Up for Security and Privacy. *Proceedings of the IEEE*, 108(2):373–389, 2020.

2

Trust Management Meets the Internet of Vehicles

Recent technological breakthroughs in vehicular ad hoc networks and the Internet of Things (IoT) have transformed vehicles into smart objects thus paving the way for the evolution of the promising paradigm of the Internet of Vehicles (IoV), which is an integral constituent of the modern intelligent transportation systems. Simply put, IoV attributes to the *IoT-on-wheels*, wherein vehicles broadcast safety-critical information among one another (and their immediate ambiences) for guaranteeing highly reliable and efficacious traffic flows. This, therefore, necessitates the need to fully secure an IoV network since a single malicious message is capable enough of jeopardizing the safety of the nearby vehicles (and their respective passengers) and vulnerable pedestrians. It is also pertinent to mention that a malicious attacker; i.e., vehicle, is not only able to send counterfeited safety-critical messages to its nearby vehicles and the traffic management authorities but could further enable a compromised vehicle to broadcast both spoofed coordinates and speed-related information. It is, therefore, of the utmost importance that malicious entities and their messages be identified and subsequently eliminated from the network before they are able to manipulate the entire network for their malicious gains. This chapter, therefore, delineates on the convergence of the notion of trust with the IoV primarily in terms of its underlying rationale. It further highlights the opportunities which transpire as a result of this convergence to secure an IoV network. Finally, open research challenges, together with the recommendations for addressing the same, have been discussed.

2.1 Introduction

Over the past decade or so, significant cutting-edge technological advancements in the promising paradigm of vehicular ad hoc networks and the Internet of Things (IoT) have led to the emergence of the Internet of Vehicles (IoV) as a highly innovative technology, which has the potential of revolutionizing the intelligent transportation systems that are indispensable for the realization of the futuristic smart cities [1]. Intelligent IoV networks are capable of

DOI: 10.1201/9781003365037-2

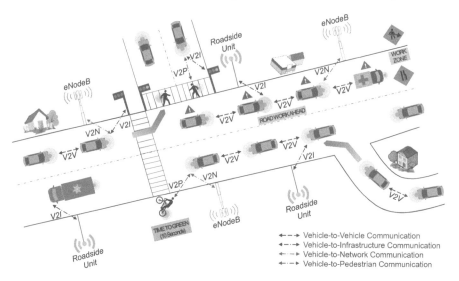

FIGURE 2.1
An overview of V2X communication in an IoV landscape.

ensuring highly secure and safe traffic flows on the road by empowering smart vehicles duly equipped with storage and computational resources and next generation communication technologies for communicating safety-critical information with the (a) other vehicles in their neighborhood, (b) supporting roadside infrastructure, (c) backbone network, and (d) pedestrians via Vehicle to Everything (V2X) communication [2, 3]. It is pertinent to highlight that the safety-critical vehicular applications have strict performance requirements in contrast to the non-safety, i.e., infotainment, applications, and hence, a low-latency and highly secure IoV network is quite imperative for the same [4]. Figure 2.1 depicts an overview of V2X communication in an IoV landscape.

However, just like other ad hoc networks, IoV networks are prone to a number of external and internal security threats [5], and in fact, a single malicious message possesses the capability to compromise the entire network, thereby putting human lives to risk on the road. It is, therefore, indispensable to ensure that the malicious messages and the vehicles broadcasting them in an IoV network are identified within a shortest possible time and subsequently eliminated in an intelligent manner. Thus, the issues pertinent to the security of the IoV networks have gained a considerable level of attention of researchers from academia and industry [6]. As of date, the existing security solutions are categorized into two categories, i.e., cryptographic-based solutions and trust-based solutions. Cryptographic-based solutions usually employ certificates and public key infrastructure for the purpose of vehicles' identification and guarantee that messages are broadcast from the authenticated vehicles, however, they are unable to inhibit any legitimate vehicle from broadcasting false information [7, 8]. It is owing to this reason that the notion of trust was lately introduced in the literature for tackling insider attacks in an IoV network.

Trust within an IoV network is referred to as the confidence of a vehicle, i.e., trustor, over the other vehicle's, i.e., trustee's, capability to share authentic, accurate, and reliable information [8, 9]. It has also been delineated in the research literature in terms of the belief of a trustor in any trustee for intelligently performing a certain task, or the sets of tasks, in an anticipated manner and perhaps within a particular time period [10]. Trust is generally ascertained in terms of the trust components and is usually an amalgamation of the direct trust and indirect trust for each vehicle. Direct trust manifests the direct observation of a trustor for a trustee, whereas, the indirect trust depicts the recommendations (opinions) of remaining one-hop neighbors in the immediate ambience of a trustee, i.e., target vehicle. The resulting trust score primarily depends on the weights assigned to each of the trust components and the quantification of these weights in its own essence is an intricate challenge since only precise weights could result in the accurate trust values. Also, trust is a dynamic entity and depends on numerous key factors, including but not limited to, the trustor's expectation over time, divergent traffic contexts, and varied applications and services. Moreover, once the aggregated trust has been ascertained for a trustee, an optimal threshold needs to be determined to identify the malicious vehicles, i.e., vehicles which satisfy the optimal threshold would be regarded as trustworthy, whereas, the ones below the optimal threshold are considered as untrustworthy in their nature. Hence, an optimal threshold is of the essence as if set too high would result in elimination of the trustworthy vehicles. Contrarily, if the optimal threshold is quite low, it would facilitate the untrustworthy vehicles to continue manipulating the IoV network for their malicious gains [11]. Unfortunately, the existing trust-based solutions have not delineated on these and a number of other IoV-related challenges in an appropriate manner.

In light of the aforementioned discussions, the chapter-at-hand delineates at length the convergence of the notion of trust with the IoV in terms of not only its underlying rationale but also by highlighting the salient opportunities it offers for strengthening the security of an IoV network along with the challenges which should be intelligently addressed for realizing the deployments of trusted IoV networks in the context of the smart cities [12].

2.2   Trust Management in the Internet of Vehicles

2.2.1   Characteristics of an IoV Network

Whilst there are a considerable number of trust management mechanisms that can ascertain the trustworthiness of *users* and *things* within a traditional ad hoc wireless network, intelligent, efficacious, resilient, and scalable trust management solutions are particularly required for IoV primarily owing to its specific characteristics some of which are delineated below [13, 14]:

- Dynamicity – In contrast to traditional MANETs, vehicles in an IoV network are highly dynamic in their nature and traverse at diverse speeds, thereby resulting in a continual change of network topology. This further suggests that the neighbors of any particular vehicle are not permanent and the trust scores are usually ascertained via merely a single encounter instead of being frequently updated over time. Bootstrapping, therefore, is of a considerable significance in an IoV network and needs to be handled carefully.

- Resource Availability – Each vehicle in an IoV network possesses certain computation and storage resources and is primarily reliant on the same for carrying out a number of its safety-critical decisions based on the data accumulated through hundreds of onboard sensors. Furthermore, it is pertinent to highlight here that vehicles also offload data both to the edge and to the centralized clouds for the purposes of heavy computation, nevertheless, this comes at a cost of compromising stringent latency requirements and which are, in fact, highly indispensable for the successful realization of the safety-critical vehicular applications.

- Regulated – Vehicles in an IoV network are obligated to follow traffic regulations put forth by both the centralized and localized traffic management entities, and are further bounded by the road topologies.

- Opportunistic – Vehicles are opportunistic in nature since they are intermittently connected with the other vehicles, pedestrians, and the roadside infrastructure. This implies that vehicles interact with the other vehicles, pedestrians, and the roadside infrastructure if they fall in the communication range of one another.

- Non-deterministic – Unlike a deterministic behavior that could be easily related to its cause and is, therefore, predictable (i.e., just as is the case of deterministic networks, wherein an event could be guaranteed to transpire within a particular duration of time), the IoV networks somehow possess non-deterministic characteristics primarily owing to the complicated nature of its entities and their intricate interrelationships. Although the mobility of the vehicles is generally predictable in IoV networks, it is the intelligent dishonest vehicles which remain in disguise, attains sufficient privileges, find an optimal opportunity for launching a sophisticated attack, and jeopardizes the entire network in a matter of no time.

2.2.2   The Essence of Trust Management in IoV

As discussed earlier, vehicles within an IoV network communicate (interact) with one another in an attempt to carry out several safety-critical and non-safety vehicular applications. It is, therefore, indispensable that the recipient of such messages are absolutely certain about the quality of those messages, and the vehicles disseminating them, before any sort of subsequent action or decision is taken on the same. For instance, consider the safety-critical applications such as (a) a hazardous location alert intimating any vehicle of a potentially hazardous situation along its anticipated trajectory, and accordingly, recommending it to speed down and diverge towards an alternate route, or (b) a forward collision warning detecting and intimating of imminent collision, and therefore, recommending the emergency brakes to avoid any fatal accident. If the received messages are authentic, accurate, and reliable, a connected or an autonomous vehicle has to either take an alternate route in the scenario of a hazardous alert or has to apply sudden brakes for mitigating an imminent crash in the case of a forward collision alert. On the contrary, if the received messages are inauthentic, inaccurate, and unreliable, and a connected or an autonomous vehicle is unable to ascertain the same and ends up heeding to the wrong information contained therein, then it would either diverge on an unwarranted route, or alternatively, an unwarranted sudden brake on a fast moving highway would be resulting into rear-end collisions and unfortunate road fatalities.

Whilst a number of cryptographic-based solutions have been proposed in the research literature [8, 15, 16], nevertheless, cryptographic-based solutions on their own are unable to tackle the entire vehicular security aspects, and particularly, the inside attackers since they are in possession of valid certificates, have a considerable knowledge of the network, are insidious in their nature, and, therefore, can cause a catastrophic damage. Trust-based solutions are hence considered as an additional security mechanism in order to overcome the inherent shortcomings of the cryptographic-based solutions. Literature also suggests that the cryptographic-based solutions and the trust-based solutions could be employed to tackle a single attacker or even a group of attackers, and rational and irrational attacks [17]. However, the cryptographic-based solutions have high network overhead and are known for introducing excessive delays in contrast to the trust-based solutions and are, therefore, not optimal for the delay sensitive safety-critical vehicular applications.

Trust, as one of the solutions for realizing security in IoV, still remains in its infancy. In an IoV environment, the rationale behind the trust models is to guarantee a trusted dissemination of the data by identifying and subsequently revoking malicious vehicles and the compromised messages generated from them. Trust models are particularly categorized into (a) entity-centric trust models, (b) data-centric trust models, and (c) hybrid trust models, and a brief illustration pertinent to them is delineated as follows [18, 19, 20]:

- Entity-centric Trust Models – Entity-centric trust models primarily intend to eliminate the malicious vehicles from an IoV network by ascertaining the trustworthiness of the vehicles (entities) disseminating messages. They rely on a reputation-based trust evaluation mechanism, and hence, the opinions from the neighboring vehicles are taken into consideration in order to ascertain the trustworthiness of the source vehicles.

- Data-centric Trust Models – Contrary to the entity-centric trust models, data-centric trust models intend to eliminate the malicious messages from an IoV network instead of eliminating the vehicles. This could be, therefore, realized in two ways, i.e., either the messages disseminated by the malicious vehicles could be eliminated or messages could be verified provided they are not encrypted.

- Hybrid Trust Models – Hybrid trust models encompass the characteristics of both the entity-centric trust models and the data-centric trust models. Accordingly, the trustworthiness of both the vehicles and the data disseminated via them is ascertained.

It is also pertinent to note that a number of trust management mechanisms primarily falling into one of the above stipulated categories have already been proposed in the research literature and leverages either the game theory, blockchain, fuzzy logic, machine learning, or other similar approaches. An overview of such schemes is beyond the scope of this chapter. Nevertheless, the readers may like to refer to our recent survey [21] depicting the state-of-the-art of trust management in IoV.

2.2.3   Trust Attributes

Trust attributes are considered as one of the most indispensable constituents of a trust-based solution. They are essentially the quality metrics which facilitate the vehicles in ascertaining the trust of any other vehicle within an IoV network. The more the number of trust attributes employed by a trustor in the trust computation process, the more accurate would be the resulting trust segment. However, too many trust attributes also implies introducing a considerable computational overhead which can prove risky in safety-critical vehicular scenarios. Therefore, it is imperative to identify the influential trust attributes that can facilitate a trustor in ascertaining an accurate trust score of a trustee in a shortest possible time. Some of such attributes that should be a part of any trust-based IoV solution are delineated as follows:

- Similarity – Similarity generally implies the state of being similar in terms of a particular aspect. The same is true for the IoV networks, wherein similarity has been ascertained in two different ways, i.e., how well the traveling patterns of a trustor resembles to that of a trustee, and the degree of similar content or services accessed by both the trustor and the trustee [22, 23].

- Familiarity – Familiarity delineates a close acquaintance with something. In simpler terms, the more knowledge we possess about something, the more aware we are with the characteristics of that particular thing. In an IoV network, familiarity suggests how well a trustor is acquainted with a trustee and is ascertained in terms of the frequency of the interactions between a trustor and a trustee [24]. It has also been ascertained via subjective logic which employs opinions for representing subjective beliefs and models belief, disbelief, uncertainty, and base rate, wherein belief and disbelief suggest a measure of the degree of trust and distrust of a trustor in a trustee, respectively; uncertainty refers to the confidence of a trustor's knowledge pertinent to a trustee, and base rate here implies the willingness of a trustor to believe in a trustee [25, 26].

- Timeliness – Timeliness is one of the most indispensable attributes in determining the trust of a trustee and is ascertained in terms of the freshness of a reputation segment. The more fresh is the reputation segment, the more recent behavior of a trustee could be established. This, therefore, could be employed to identify the presence of a malicious vehicle within an IoV network. For instance, an intelligent malicious vehicle with historically low trust scores might attract high trust scores as it begins to actively participate in the network in its disguise mode. Accordingly, the most recent reputation segments are usually compared with the previous reputation segments to trace the abrupt patterns. On the contrary, in the case of honest vehicles, the recent reputation segments are issued a relatively higher weight as compared to the old reputation segments primarily for the purpose of trust aggregation. This, in turn, provides a much clearer situation pertinent to the current state of the honest vehicles and subsequently facilitates in deciding as to which ones of those could be used for primarily routing safety-critical information in an IoV network [27, 28, 29].

- Duration of the Interactions – The duration of an interaction between a trustor and a trustee is of the essence since it is proportional to the cooperative behavior between the two. The longer is the duration of an interaction between a trustor and a trustee, the more conclusive trust score of a trustee could be ascertained. On the contrary, the shorter time a trustor and a trustee spend interacting between one another, the less knowledge a trustor possess pertinent to a trustee's behavior and strengths [30].

- Effective Distance – Effective distance between a trustor and a trustee is yet another intelligent geographical measure to ascertain the trust of a trustee reporting a particular event. The greater is the distance between a trustor and a trustee reporting an event, the more improbable it would be for a trustor and it's immediate neighbors to ascertain the legitimacy of the said event. Contrarily, if the distance between a trustor and a trustee reporting a certain event is less, the trustor and its immediate neighbors would be capable of attesting the legitimacy of the said event since they are much likely to be aware of the events transpiring in their message evaluation range [1, 31].

If carefully observed, these trust attributes are pretty similar to the ones that humans employ for ascertaining the trust of the other humans.

Surprisingly enough, there is a sharp similarity between the two and this makes perfect sense since trust is an intrinsic characteristic of humans and which subconsciously is also reflected in their engineered trust models. This, therefore, implies that some additional influential trust attributes for IoVs could be extracted from the domain of human behavior which has been well researched for numerous decades. A comparison of the trust attributes in humans vis-à-vis IoV is illustrated in Table 2.1.

2.2.4   Trust-Related Attacks in an IoV Network

There are numerous sorts of sophisticated attacks that could have a direct impact on the trustworthiness of any vehicle in an IoV network. Such sorts of attacks include (a) self-promoting attacks, on-off attacks, opportunistic service attacks, selective behavior attacks – manifesting the class of attacks with the underlying rationale of *self-interest*; and (b) bad mouthing attacks and good mouthing attacks – classified as the *reputation-based attacks*. These attacks are briefly delineated as follows:

- Self-promoting Attack – In a self-promoting attack, a malicious vehicle continuously enhances its own reputation for acquiring considerable privileges in an IoV network in a bid to manipulate the entire network for its malicious gains. In order to materialize such an attack, a malicious vehicle can generate Sybil identities to augment its trust, thereby cheating the conventional reputation mechanisms.

- On-off Attack – In an on-off attack, a malicious vehicle alters between a good and a bad behavior in a randomized manner. This not only facilitates a malicious vehicle as to remain undetected while engaging in malign activities but further guarantees that it is able to manage an appropriate reputation score in an IoV network. If remains undetected for an extended duration, such sort of malicious vehicles may end up gaining significant privileges in the network.

- Opportunistic Service Attack – In an opportunistic service attack, a malicious vehicle lay quite low by acting primarily in disguise mode until it has been presented with some sort of an opportunity for launching a sophisticated attack in an IoV network. Therefore, a malicious vehicle keeps on providing a better service as to gain a higher reputation and perhaps the trust of its neighboring vehicles, and once it has duly established the same, it acts opportunistically and begins furnishing the bad services.

- Selective Behavior Attack – In a selective behavior attack, a malicious vehicle performs good for a particular set of services, whereas, bad for the others. For instance, in the case of network services demanding lower computational requirements, a malicious vehicle might perform good in order to preserve its key resources in an IoV network. It is pertinent to highlight

TABLE 2.1

A comparison of the trust attributes in humans vis-à-vis the Internet of Vehicles.

Attribute	Humans	Internet of Vehicles
Similarity	Similarity amongst the behavior of two humans is primarily ascertained in terms of their biases (personal preferences – likes and dislikes), rationale for such personal preferences, emotional reactions, decision making, cultures, friends, etc.	Similarity in vehicles is measured in terms of (a) how well the traveling patterns of a trustor and a trustee resembles to one another, or (b) the degree of similar content or services accessed by both the trustor and the trustee.
Familiarity	Humans, unconsciously, tend to accord preference to other humans that they are usually familiar with. In fact, the more often a human sees another human, the more attraction they tend to develop over time. Even if the stimuli they are being exposed to overtime is itself negative, humans tend to find comfort in the familiarity of the same. Hence, humans don't risk the unfamiliar owing to the fear of getting hurt.	Familiarity between any two vehicles manifest how well a trustor is acquainted with a trustee and is measured in terms of the frequency of interactions between them. It has also been ascertained in terms of the degree of trust and distrust of a trustor on a trustee, confidence of a trustor's knowledge pertinent to a trustee, and willingness of a trustor to believe in a trustee.
Timeliness	Human behavior primarily relates to the way a human act or interact with other humans in its ambient environment and is dependent on and influenced by a number of factors. It can change gradually and even drastically, and therefore, humans tend to believe more in the recent observations and interactions as compared to the historical ones.	Timeliness in an IoV network implies freshness of any reputation segment. The more fresh is the reputation segment, the more recent behavior of a vehicle could be ascertained. This is of key essence since the recent reputation segments could be matched with the historical ones to figure out any abnormal behavior.
Duration of Interactions	Humans truly believe in the duration of their interactions since this is largely known to facilitate them in ascertaining the strength of their relationship, and in turn, the feasibility of continuing the same. This is the most important attribute as other trust attributes are somehow impacted owing to it.	In an IoV network, the longer is the duration of any interaction amongst a trustor and a trustee, the more conclusive trust score of a trustee can be ascertained. This assessment could be positive or negative, and in fact, computationally intensive but indisputable for making a judgment.
Effective Distance	Long-distance relationships amongst humans are somewhat prone to failure. The greater is the distance among any two individuals, the less likely they are able to relate over time with one another.	The greater is the distance between a trustor and a trustee reporting a particular event, the more improbable it would be for a trustor (and it's immediate neighbors) to ascertain legitimacy of the event.

here that vehicles in a collaborative network cooperate with one another in a bid to facilitate the network to execute its services in an efficient manner, and accordingly, justify their due participation within this process. Hence, even with a selective behavior, wherein a malicious vehicle turns down the cooperation for computational intensive services, it is still able to maintain a reasonable level of reputation for itself in an IoV network.

- Bad-mouthing Attack – In the scenario of a bad-mouthing attack, malicious vehicles deliberately furnish a bad reputation to the trustworthy vehicles in an attempt to damage their reputation in an IoV network. This, thus, minimizes the probability of the trustworthy vehicles to acquire their due privileges in an IoV network. Bad-mouthing attacks are generally sophisticated in nature as malicious vehicles intelligent collude with one another with the key intent to target the trustworthy vehicles, thereby eliminating them out of an IoV network over time.

- Ballot Stuffing Attack – In the case of a ballot stuffing attack, the malicious vehicles collude with one another in a bid to enhance the trustworthiness of another malicious vehicle in an IoV network. The risk manifolds if the malicious vehicle, i.e., whose reputation has been augmented, ends up becoming a cluster head in a cluster as this could jeopardize the safety of not only the occupants of vehicles but also the vulnerable pedestrians.

2.3   Research Challenges and Future Prospects

Although the notion of trust has been well researched over the past decade, its convergence with the promising paradigm of IoV still remains in its infancy primarily owing to a number of bottlenecks. Accordingly, in this section, we have identified several such bottlenecks together with some probable solutions to expedite the true realization of a trusted IoV network in the context of the futuristic smart cities.

2.3.1   Lifetime of the Trust Score

As discussed earlier, vehicles in an IoV network are required to keep a record of the trust scores of all the other vehicles with which they have interacted during their respective trajectories. Unlike static networks, the IoV networks are highly dynamic in their nature, and consequently, vehicles usually come across hundreds and thousands of other vehicles within their immediate neighborhood once they traverse along the roads. However, vehicles possess limited onboard storage, and keeping in view a number of important operations that simultaneously transpire within the connected and autonomous vehicles with competing storage requirements, it is not only impossible but impractical for any vehicle to store the trust scores of all of its neighboring vehicles for an extended time period. Hence, it is indispensable to decide on the duration for which a vehicle should record the trust score of its neighboring vehicles in a given context since a vehicle may interact with some vehicles frequently over time but may never encounter others again. For instance, vehicles in dense traffic conditions are expected to come across frequently as opposed to those within sparse traffic conditions. Similarly, vehicles traveling to a similar destination or to the destinations which fall along a similar trajectory have a higher probability of coming in contact with one another. Hence, context-aware schemes that are capable of intelligently deciding an optimal duration for which a vehicle should maintain the record of the trust score of a neighboring vehicle (that it has interacted with) need to be devised and deployed in a trust-based IoV network.

2.3.2 Decay in the Trust Score

As discussed earlier, the trust score of a vehicle is dependent on the quality of its interactions with the neighboring vehicles in an IoV network. Furthermore, the trust score of a vehicle is frequently updated as long as it remains in an interactive mode; i.e., the trust score gets incremented or decremented primarily depending on its respective interacting behavior. Nevertheless, the trust of a vehicle should also be subject to some form of a decay if it has not come in an interaction with any other vehicle for a certain duration of time. This is of key essence in order to ensure fairness in the trust system since vehicles which violate the intrinsic collaborative behavior of an IoV network (wherein vehicles cooperate in the traffic routing mechanisms or at least have willingness to cooperate in the routing mechanism) needs to be penalized to a certain extent. Therefore, it is imperative to come up with a decay strategy that would allow the network to penalize the trust score of such a vehicle by a certain factor. Literature suggests that similar decaying strategies have been proposed for conventional social IoT networks [10, 32] and the same could be appropriately tweaked for IoV networks; however, the real challenge lies in deciding the factor by which a trust score has to decay. Existing research in the domain of IoV has yet not accounted for the same in its true essence. Hence, appropriate trust management policies need to devised and subsequently implemented in this regard.

2.3.3 Incentivizing Selfish Vehicles

Similar to some humans which are classified as being selfish primarily owing to their ulterior motives, vehicles may possess a selfish behavior too. Selfish vehicles are usually referred to as the ones that opt not to interact with their neighboring vehicles on a continual basis, i.e., they only participate within a network when it best suits their interests, and in that occurrence, might interact actively so as to build a favorable reputation in an IoV network in a bid to attain privileges. Such a selective behavior, in turn, degrades the combined trust evaluation mechanism in an IoV network since the recommendation of the neighboring nodes, i.e., indirect trust, is essential for evaluating a particular node. It is, therefore, indispensable to incentivize such vehicles for stimulating their participation in an IoV network. Although a number of incentivization mechanisms have been envisaged over the years within the research literature, nevertheless, they need to be considerably tweaked for addressing the highly non-deterministic behavior of IoV networks. In fact, a careful study of the selfish behavior in humans would undoubtedly facilitate in devising better incentivization strategies for the trust-based IoV networks too.

2.3.4 Adaptive Trust Thresholds

It is pertinent to highlight here that the existing trust-based IoV mechanisms engage a pre-defined static threshold to determine the trustworthiness of a vehicle in an IoV network, i.e., as either trustworthy or untrustworthy in nature. Nevertheless, the static thresholds deliberated in the existing literature have no underlying rationale with a number of trust-based mechanisms evaluating the trustworthiness against varied thresholds. If the said threshold is set too high, it would result in the elimination of the honest vehicles. On the contrary, if this threshold is set too low, it would facilitate the malicious vehicles to manipulate the IoV network for an extended period of time. Even if a static threshold has been optimally calculated and then subsequently set, the intelligent malicious vehicles could still manipulate it for their malicious gains; i.e., an intelligent malicious vehicle could act malicious for a certain duration of time, and as soon as it realizes that its trust evaluation has started dropping and is near to the static threshold, it could go into disguise by acting honestly, thereby gaining trust in an IoV network. Hence, it is indispensable to devise an adaptive threshold mechanism that is capable of identifying the intelligent malicious vehicles once they are busy pursuing malicious activities in an attacking time window so that they could be eliminated from an IoV network in a timely manner.

However, there are a number of bottlenecks that may impede the realization of such adaptive threshold mechanisms since it is extremely inefficient to continuously monitor and adjust the adaptive threshold of each vehicle within an IoV network, and particularly, in dense scenarios. One possible alternative could be to instigate an adaptive threshold only when the trust score of a particular vehicle falls within an inspection threshold; i.e., an inspection threshold is a threshold in a certain range of the original (base) threshold and plays the role of a trigger.

2.3.5 Trust-Based IoV Threat Models

An overarching and a realistic threat model is of the essence in a bid to carefully examine the structural vulnerabilities of an IoV network, attackers' profiles in terms of their complex sets of attributes along with their probable dynamic attack vectors under varying contexts, and the absence of optimal safeguards in an IoV environment that should have been put into place for mitigating the impacts of adversaries. It is extremely pertinent to mention that such threat models are completely non-existent in the domain of IoV and should be devised and subsequently improved over time in view of any emerging threats.

2.3.6 Trust-Based IoV Testbed

As-of-date, the existing trust-based IoV solutions employed different simulation tools, including but not limited to, Veins[1], SUMO[2], OMNeT++[3], network simulator 3[4], VanetMobiSim[5], ONE simulator[6], and mobility simulators programmed in Java, MATLAB, and Python, for evaluating the performance of their respective trust models. Whilst a number of these simulations are comprehensive on their own, the simulators employed do not capture well the true essence of an IoV environment. Also, the existing trust-based IoV solutions have employed different trust attributes for ascertaining the trust scores of the vehicles and additionally measured their performance against somewhat a varying sets of metrics too. A realistic testbed is, therefore, indispensable for evaluating and comparing these trust models and to subsequently come up with an optimum solution. Also, designing of such testbeds is a complicated task on its own. It is interesting to note that trust testbeds have started appearing within the research literature for the social IoT networks [33], and although they cannot be employed for the IoV networks, they could still serve as a guidance for conceiving testbeds for the highly dynamic IoV environments.

2.3.7 Digital Twins and the Resiliency of the Trust-Based IoV Networks

The notion of digital twins has lately emerged as one of the disruptive technologies for addressing a number of challenges of the automotive sector [34, 35]. It is refereed to as a digital representation of any physical entity which has the ability to be continuously updated via a real-time data, and uses simulation, machine learning, and reasoning ability for intelligent decision making

---

[1] https://veins.car2x.org/
[2] https://www.eclipse.org/sumo/
[3] https://omnetpp.org/
[4] https://www.nsnam.org/
[5] https://www.eurecom.fr/publication/2220
[6] https://akeranen.github.io/the-one/

purposes. To put simply, it facilitates in simulating the proposed models much ahead of their implementation, thereby unveiling complex problems before they even become a reality. In the case of IoV, digital twins can be employed for simulating the malicious behaviors of an unwarranted intruder in a bid to develop intelligent decision making and appropriate mitigation strategies to detect, and accordingly, respond to such malicious behaviors. This subsequently facilitates the system designers to test diverse sets of simultaneous trust-based attacks along with the attackers' dynamic strategies vis-à-vis diversified contexts. However, for this to transpire well, the digital twins themselves need to be protected first. For instance, digital twin of a smart city traffic management relies on the data streams accumulated from several end points, i.e., IoT sensors, and each of this end point may prove vulnerable to various attacks if not equipped with robust security mechanisms. Hence, it is indispensable to devise and deploy secure digital twins so that they could be of essence in strengthening the resiliency of the trust-based IoV networks.

2.4 Summary

A secure and trusted environment is extremely indispensable for the realization of futuristic smart cities, wherein connected and autonomous vehicles are expected to be the primary mode of personal and commercial transportation, and whose success is primarily dependent on factors such as the resiliency of the IoV networks and the dissemination of authentic, accurate, and reliable information within the same. Trust, in this regard, can play its strategic role by strengthening the resiliency of an IoV network, in particular, against the insider attacks. This chapter, thus, delineates on the convergence of trust with the IoV networks primarily in terms of its underlying rationale, highlights the opportunities that transpire as a result of this convergence, and finally, discusses the open research challenges along with some key recommendations.

Bibliography

[1] Farhan Ahmad, Fatih Kurugollu, Chaker Kerrache, Sakir Sezer, and Lu Liu. NOTRINO: A NOvel Hybrid TRust Management Scheme for INternet-of-Vehicles. *IEEE Transactions on Vehicular Technology*, 70(9):9244–9257, 2021.

[2] Adnan Mahmood, Wei Emma Zhang, and Quan Z. Sheng. Software-defined Heterogeneous Vehicular Networking: The Architectural Design and Open Challenges. *Future Internet*, 11(3):70, 2019.

[3] Aljawharah Alnasser, Hongjian Sun, and Jing Jiang. Recommendation-based Trust Model for Vehicle-to-Everything (V2X). *IEEE Internet of Things Journal*, 7(1):440–450, 2020.

[4] Carlos Renato Storck and Fátima Duarte-Figueiredo. A 5G V2X Ecosystem Providing Internet of Vehicles. *Sensors*, 19(3):550, 2019.

[5] Jiliang Li, Rui Xing, Zhou Su, Ning Zhang, Yilong Hui, Tom H. Luan, and Hangguan Shan. Trust Based Secure Content Delivery in Vehicular Networks: A Bargaining Game Theoretical Approach. *IEEE Transactions on Vehicular Technology*, 69(3):3267–3279, 2020.

[6] Shirin Abbasi, Amir Rahmani, Ali Balador, and Amir Sahafi. Internet of Vehicles: Architecture, Services, and Applications. *International Journal of Communication Systems*, 34(10):e4793, 2021.

[7] Farhan Ahmad, Virginia Franqueira, and Asma Adnane. TEAM: A Trust Evaluation and Management Framework in Context-Enabled Vehicular Ad-Hoc Networks. *IEEE Access*, 6:28643–28660, 2018.

[8] Shrikant Tangade, Sunilkumar Manvi, and Pascal Lorenz. Trust Management Scheme Based on Hybrid Cryptography for Secure Communications in VANETs. *IEEE Transactions on Vehicular Technology*, 69(5):5232–5243, 2020.

[9] Adnan Mahmood, Bernard Butler, Wei Emma Zhang, Quan Z. Sheng, and Sarah Ali Siddiqui. A Hybrid Trust Management Heuristic for VANETs. In *2019 IEEE International Conference on Pervasive Computing and Communications Workshops (PerCom Workshops)*, pages 748–752, 2019.

[10] Nguyen B. Truong, Tai-Won Um, Bo Zhou, and Gyu Myoung Lee. From Personal Experience to Global Reputation for Trust Evaluation in the Social Internet of Things. In *GLOBECOM 2017-2017 IEEE Global Communications Conference*, pages 1–7, 2017.

[11] Chaker Abdelaziz Kerrache, Nasreddine Lagraa, Rasheed Hussain, Syed Hassan Ahmed, Abderrahim Benslimane, Carlos T. Calafate, Juan-Carlos Cano, and Anna Maria Vegni. TACASHI: Trust-Aware Communication Architecture for Social Internet of Vehicles. *IEEE Internet of Things Journal*, 6(4):5870–5877, 2019.

[12] Adnan Mahmood, Quan Z. Sheng, Sarah Ali Siddiqui, Subhash Sagar, Wei Emma Zhang, Hajime Suzuki, and Wei Ni. When Trust Meets the Internet of Vehicles: Opportunities, Challenges, and Future Prospects. In *2021 IEEE 7th International Conference on Collaboration and Internet Computing (CIC)*, pages 60–67, Atlanta, GA, USA, 2021. IEEE.

[13] Rasheed Hussain, Jooyoung Lee, and Sherali Zeadally. Trust in VANET – A Survey of Current Solutions and Future Research Opportunities. *IEEE Transactions on Intelligent Transportation Systems*, 22(5):2553–2571, 2021.

[14] Muhammad Tahir Abbas, Afaq Muhammad, and Wang-Cheol Song. SD-IoV: SDN Enabled Routing for Internet of Vehicles in Road-aware Approach. *Journal of Ambient Intelligence and Humanized Computing*, 11(3):1265–1280, 2020.

[15] Chuan Zhang, Liehuang Zhu, Chang Xu, Kashif Sharif, Kai Ding, Ximeng Liu, Xiaojiang Du, and Mohsen Guizani. TPPR: A Trust-Based and Privacy-Preserving Platoon Recommendation Scheme in VANET. *IEEE Transactions on Services Computing*, 2019.

[16] Ricardo Mühlbauer and João Henrique Kleinschmidt. Bring Your Own Reputation: A Feasible Trust System for Vehicular Ad Hoc Networks. *Journal of Sensor and Actuator Networks*, 7(3):37, 2018.

[17] Chaker Abdelaziz Kerrache, Carlos T. Calafate, Juan-Carlos Cano, Nasreddine Lagraa, and Pietro Manzoni. Trust Management for Vehicular Networks: An Adversary-Oriented Overview. *IEEE Access*, 4:9293–9307, 2016.

[18] Adnan Mahmood, Wei Emma Zhang, Quan Z Sheng, Sarah Siddiqui, and Abdulwahab Aljubairy. Trust Management for Software-Defined Heterogeneous Vehicular Ad Hoc Networks. In Zaigham Mahmood, editor, *Security, Privacy and Trust in the IoT Environment*, pages 203–226. Springer International Publishing, Cham, Switzerland, 2019.

[19] Jinsong Zhang, Kangfeng Zheng, Dongmei Zhang, and Bo Yan. AATMS: An Anti-Attack Trust Management Scheme in VANET. *IEEE Access*, 8:21077–21090, 2020.

[20] Muhammad Sohail, Rashid Ali, Muhammad Kashif, Sher Ali, Sumet Mehta, Yousaf Bin Zikria, and Heejung Yu. TrustWalker: An Efficient Trust Assessment in Vehicular Internet of Things (VIoT) with Security Consideration. *Sensors*, 20(14):3945, 2020.

[21] Sarah Ali Siddiqui, Adnan Mahmood, Quan Z Sheng, Hajime Suzuki, and Wei Ni. A Survey of Trust Management in the Internet of Vehicles. *Electronics*, 10(18):2223, 2021.

[22] Adnan Mahmood, Sarah Ali Siddiqui, Wei Emma Zhang, and Quan Z. Sheng. A Hybrid Trust Management Model for Secure and Resource Efficient Vehicular Ad hoc Networks. In *20th International Conference on Parallel and Distributed Computing, Applications, and Technologies (PDCAT)*, pages 154–159, 2019.

[23] Sarah Ali Siddiqui, Adnan Mahmood, Wei Emma Zhang, and Quan Z Sheng. Machine Learning Based Trust Model for Misbehaviour Detection in Internet-of-Vehicles. In Tom Gedeon, Kok Wai Wong, and Minho Lee, editors, *Neural Information Processing*, pages 512–520, Cham, 2019. Springer International Publishing.

[24] Hui Xia, Fu Xiao, San-shun Zhang, Chun-qiang Hu, and Xiu-zhen Cheng. Trustworthiness Inference Framework in the Social Internet of Things: A Context-Aware Approach. In *IEEE INFOCOM 2019 – IEEE Conference on Computer Communications*, pages 838–846, 2019.

[25] Xumin Huang, Rong Yu, Jiawen Kang, and Yan Zhang. Distributed Reputation Management for Secure and Efficient Vehicular Edge Computing and Networks. *IEEE Access*, 5:25408–25420, 2017.

[26] Besat Jafarian, Nasser Yazdani, and Mohammad Sayad Haghighi. Discrimination-aware Trust Management for Social Internet of Things. *Computer Networks*, 178:107254, 2020.

[27] M. Raya, P. Papadimitratos, V. D. Gligor, and J.-P. Hubaux. On Data-Centric Trust Establishment in Ephemeral Ad Hoc Networks. In *IEEE INFOCOM 2008 - The 27th Conference on Computer Communications*, pages 1238–1246, 2008.

[28] Razi Iqbal, Talal Ashraf Butt, Muhammad Afzaal, and Khaled Salah. Trust Management in Social Internet of Vehicles: Factors, Challenges, Blockchain, and Fog Solutions. *International Journal of Distributed Sensor Networks*, 15(1), 2019.

[29] Hamssa Hasrouny, Abed Ellatif Samhat, Carole Bassil, and Anis Laouiti. Trust Model for Secure Group Leader-based Communications in VANET. *Wireless Networks*, 25(8):4639–4661, 2019.

[30] Upul Jayasinghe, Gyu Myoung Lee, Tai-Won Um, and Qi Shi. Machine Learning Based Trust Computational Model for IoT Services. *IEEE Transactions on Sustainable Computing*, 4(1):39–52, 2019.

[31] Farhan Ahmad, Fatih Kurugollu, Asma Adnane, Rasheed Hussain, and Fatima Hussain. MARINE: Man-in-the-Middle Attack Resistant Trust Model in Connected Vehicles. *IEEE Internet of Things Journal*, 7(4):3310–3322, 2020.

[32] Anuoluwapo A. Adewuyi, Hui Cheng, Qi Shi, Jiannong Cao, Xingwei Wang, and Bo Zhou. SC-TRUST: A Dynamic Model for Trustworthy Service Composition in the Internet of Things. *IEEE Internet of Things Journal*, 2021.

[33] Subhash Sagar, Adnan Mahmood, Quan Z. Sheng, and Sarah Ali Siddiqui. SCaRT-SIoT: Towards a Scalable and Robust Trust Platform for

the Social Internet of Things: Demo Abstract. In *Proceedings of the 18th International Conference on Embedded Networked Sensor Systems*, SenSys'20, page 635–636, New York, NY, USA, 2020. Association for Computing Machinery.

[34] Sadeq Almeaibed, Saba Al-Rubaye, Antonios Tsourdos, and Nicolas P. Avdelidis. Digital Twin Analysis to Promote Safety and Security in Autonomous Vehicles. *IEEE Communications Standards Magazine*, 5(1):40–46, 2021.

[35] Tianle Zhang, Xiangtao Liu, Zongwei Luo, Fuqiang Dong, and Yu Jiang. Time Series Behavior Modeling with Digital Twin for Internet of Vehicles. *EURASIP Journal on Wireless Communications and Networking*, 2019(1):271, 2019.

3

Trust – IoV: A Distributed Trust Management System for Misbehavior Detection in the Internet of Vehicles

Recent considerable state-of-the-art advancements within the automotive sector, coupled with an evolution of the promising paradigms of vehicle-to-everything communication and the Internet of Vehicles (IoV), have facilitated vehicles to generate, and accordingly, disseminate an enormous amount of safety-critical and non-safety infotainment data in a bid to guarantee a highly safe, convenient, and congestion-aware road transport. Such sort of a dynamic network requires intelligent security measures to ensure that the malicious messages, along with the vehicles that disseminate them, are identified and subsequently eliminated in a timely manner so that they are not in a position to harm other vehicles. Failing to do so could jeopardize the entire network leading to fatalities and injuries amongst road users. Several researchers, over the years, have envisaged conventional cryptographic-based solutions employing certificates and the public key infrastructure for enhancing the security of vehicular networks. Nevertheless, cryptographic-based solutions are not optimum for an IoV network primarily since the cryptographic schemes could be susceptible to poor key hygiene, compromised trust authorities, and insider attacks which are insidious, i.e., are highly deceptive in nature and cannot be noticed immediately, and are, therefore, capable of causing a catastrophic damage. Accordingly, in this chapter, a distributed trust management system has been proposed which ascertains the trust of all the reputation segments within an IoV network. The envisaged system takes into consideration the salient characteristics of familiarity, i.e., assessed via a subjective logic approach, similarity, and timeliness in order to ascertain the weights of all the reputation segments. Furthermore, an intelligent trust threshold mechanism has been developed for the identification and eviction of the misbehaving vehicles. The experimental results suggest the advantages of our proposed IoV-based trust management system in terms of optimizing the misbehavior detection and its resilience to various sorts of attacks.

DOI: 10.1201/9781003365037-3

3.1   Introduction

Over the past few decades, the transportation industry has made considerable advancements in terms of sophisticated hardware and software primarily in a bid to make vehicles more and more smart for enhancing the overall safety and convenience of their passengers. Today, the state-of-the-art connected vehicles not only interact with the other vehicles in their immediate ambience via vehicle-to-vehicle communication but also liaise with the roadside infrastructure, e.g., together with the roadside sensors, via vehicle-to-infrastructure communication and with the (vulnerable) pedestrians via vehicle-to-pedestrian communication[1] [2]. All of these ultimately result in formulating a network of intelligent devices (the *participants* of a network), thereby promulgating the promising yet emerging paradigm of Vehicle-to-Everything (V2X) communication which is the most crucial enabler for the Internet of Vehicles (IoV) primarily within the context of the intelligent transportation systems [3, 4, 5, 6]. V2X communication, in its essence, acts as a unified connectivity platform facilitating all of the road entities to periodically disseminate safety-critical information, including but not limited to, their speed, trajectory, and current location on the road. In case of any unwarranted incidents, i.e., traffic congestion or accidents, a safety-critical warning message is disseminated in a bid to alarm the vehicles of such unfortunate incidents along their respective trajectories [7]. It is pertinent to note that the static nodes generally have a stable connection and a static topology, nevertheless, mobile nodes possess inherent challenges as they are extremely dynamic in their nature, and hence, communication time between them is minimal. Furthermore, ad hoc connections between the vehicles are more susceptible to both external and internal attacks since they are not directly controlled via a core network (just as in the case of a cellular connection). External attacks generally transpire as a result of unauthorized entities and may get initialized if an honest vehicle traverses in an area that does not falls within the network coverage and interacts with a malicious vehicle. On the contrary, the internal attacks are launched by authorized vehicles with validated credentials which perhaps overcome the conventional security techniques of authentication and cryptography. Moreover, the transaction messages, i.e., encompassing both personal and confidential information, need to be securely forwarded to the core network. Nevertheless, a relaying vehicle in the form

---

[1]Vehicle-to-Pedestrian (V2P) communication is a blanket terminology encompassing communication between the vehicles and the vulnerable road users. It is pertinent to mention that pedestrians, cyclists, and two-wheeler operators are all categorized as the vulnerable road users and which primarily vary in their characteristics, i.e., the speed and traveling patterns [1]. V2P communication, therefore, facilitates the vulnerable road users to become an integral constituent of the intelligent transportation systems primarily for the purposes of cooperative safety-critical applications.

of an internal attacker may hinder the packet forwarding process, thereby affecting the network performance in an adverse manner [8, 9, 10].

Accordingly, the notion of trust management has been as of late envisaged by researchers in both academia and industry for tackling the issue of internal attacks in an IoV network. Trust management segregates messages and their respective senders into two distinct categories, i.e., malicious and the non-malicious. Trust itself is a derived quantity and is, therefore, assigned to a vehicle based on its behavior. Trust models hence facilitate by enabling a vehicle to observe other vehicles in its immediate ambience in a bid to precisely collect appropriate information about them. This information is also disseminated to the neighboring vehicles or to a localized or a centralized trust authority (depending on the underlying architecture) as recommendation for the purposes of trust aggregation [11, 12].

A wide variety of trust models have already been proposed in the research literature for ascertaining the trust of a node in a vehicular networking environment. A number of these trust-based computational models have employed some vehicles as verifiers, which upon verifying the validity of the received messages, forward the decision to the non-verified vehicles for either accepting or rejecting the messages. Other trust models have also classified vehicles as per their trustworthiness level depending on which any receiver could decide to either receive, forward, or fully drop a message. Nevertheless, in such sort of trust models, decisions pertinent to a vehicle could only be reached once any previous interaction has already been recorded with the said vehicle, and which, in fact, is not the case within an IoV network primarily owing to the highly dynamic behavior of the vehicles [13]. Furthermore, it is highly indispensable to appropriately weigh the reputation segments originating as a result of a direct interaction or received as a recommendation via the one-hop neighboring vehicles. This is particularly of essence since each observing vehicle possesses varying capabilities and diversifying conditions, i.e., at the time of observing and evaluating a targeted vehicle, thereby resulting in trust segments with diverging qualities. Hence, weighing the reputation segments in conformance with certain quality attributes is crucial for improving the overall accuracy of any trust model. Nevertheless, such an assessment of the quality attributes has been largely ignored in the existing literature.

To overcome the said limitations, in this chapter, a distributed trust management system has been developed which ascertains the trust of all the reputation segments in an IoV network. Since the accuracy of these reputation segments is of paramount significance, weights have been hence ascertained for all of the reputations segments in conformance with the prior knowledge and context possessed by the respective one-hop neighboring vehicles of a targeted vehicle (trustee). These weights take into consideration the salient characteristics of familiarity, similarity, and timeliness. Therefore, the trust segments determined for a targeted vehicle via all of these one-hop neighboring vehicles at a given time instance are appropriately aggregated in order to compute the overall trust of a targeted vehicle [14]. The performance of the envisaged IoV-based trust model has been investigated in terms of optimizing the misbehavior detection and its resilience to attacks . We summarize the key contributions of the research-at-hand as follows:

- A distributed trust computational model has been devised which accurately ascertains the trust score of a targeted vehicle by weighing its trust segments received as a result of a direct interaction (direct trust) or via recommendations from the one-hop neighboring vehicles (indirect trust). The weights of these trust segments have been ascertained by taking into consideration the characteristics of familiarity, similarity, and timeliness,

- An intelligent trust threshold mechanism has been developed which is capable of identifying and evicting the misbehaving vehicles from an IoV network in an accurate manner. The introduction of an inspection threshold, along with an allocation of additional time to vehicles being inspected under specific conditions, serve as a further check in order to guarantee that only misbehaving vehicles are eliminated from an IoV network and vehicles which are, in fact, bad-mouthed by the misbehaving vehicles can be reintegrated into the network, and

- Two different attacks, i.e., a bad-mouthing one and a self-promoting one, have been designed to ascertain the efficaciousness of the proposed trust model. The experimental results exhibit the strength of our envisaged trust model in terms of its resilience to the said attacks.

The remainder of this chapter is organized as follows. Section 3.2 delineates on the state-of-the-art of the trust management in a vehicular networking environment. Section 3.3 presents a prelude on trust management. Section 3.4 illustrates our envisaged system model and Section 3.5 reports the experimental results and theoretical analysis of the proposed system. Concluding remarks are given in Section 3.6.

3.2 The State of the Art

The promising paradigm of trust in vehicular networks has been studied for some time in the research literature. However, before we divulge deep into the same, it is pertinent to note that vehicular networks, in their essence, are a subset of Mobile Ad hoc Networks (MANETs) since the underlying principles of vehicular networks are the same as to that of the MANETs with the key differences being that (a) the nodes in a vehicular network are much more mobile in contrast to the nodes in a MANET, thereby resulting in the network topology of a vehicular network to be highly spontaneous in contrast to that of a MANET, (b) the mobility patterns of the nodes in a vehicular network are generally regular and predictable since they are constrained by the road topology, whereas, they are extremely random and unpredictable in the case of a MANET, and (c) the network density of a vehicular network could be either sparse or is often dense, whereas, a MANET is typically sparse in nature [15, 16, 17]. Over the years, a number of research studies have delineated on the notion of trust in the context of MANETs [18, 19, 20, 21], wherein numerous trust metrics, including but not limited to, throughput, overhead, goodput, packet dropping rate, utility, and delay, have been introduced in a bid to not only detect the misbehaving nodes but to mitigate the attacks instigated by them. Whilst the trust-based schemes envisaged within these MANET studies have a lot in common to that of the vehicular networks, they still cannot be directly applied to the vehicular networks owing to the above delineated differences amongst them. Below we would present an overview of the state-of-the-art of trust management in the context of the vehicular networks.

In [13], a recommendation-based trust model for the V2X network has been envisaged by the authors in order to safeguard the same against diverse sorts of attacks, i.e., routing attacks such as blackhole attacks and greyhole attacks and recommendation attacks such as bad-mouthing attacks and good-mouthing attacks, primarily to portray the non-stable, i.e., alternating, behavior of malicious attackers. An adaptive weighting heuristic has been also employed to segregate the recommendations as either positive or negative in a bid to mitigate the impact of the recommendation attacks as they possess the tendency for sending fake recommendations, thereby influencing the trust decisions. In [22], a trust evaluation and management framework for the design, management, and evaluation of trust models under numerous different contexts and primarily within the presence of malicious vehicles has been proposed by the authors. The said framework comprises five key constituents, i.e., a threat model, risk assessment, identification and classification of trust models, establishment of context, and a trust evaluation platform. The first two modules facilitate both in the identification and classification of numerous sorts of attacks, i.e., depending on the role, mobility, and impact of assets within VANETs which could be exploited by the adversaries in order to launch a malicious attack, and their criticality, i.e., depending on the likelihood of occurrence of an attack within VANETs. The remaining three modules have been employed to ascertain the efficaciousness of trust models (entity-oriented trust models, data-oriented trust models, and hybrid trust models) under dynamic contexts, i.e., depending on the high and low mobility of vehicles, and attack models, i.e., based on if the attackers are merely static or mobile in a network.

In [23], a machine learning and reputation based Misbehavior Detection System (MDS) has been envisaged for ensuring the reliability of vehicles (and their respective messages) in a 5G vehicular network. Each message is assessed for misbehavior via a machine learning-based detection system and the corresponding detection feedback obtained from each MDS is subsequently forwarded to a local authority which, in turn, is responsible for accumulating the same for each vehicle in a vehicular network via the Dempster-Shafer (DS) theory [24] so as to strengthen the detection accuracy. The results ascertained from the DS theory are further used for analyzing and updating the reputation score of a vehicle by exploiting the beta distribution. In [25], the authors suggested a secure content delivery mechanism for the vehicles requesting content from the respective roadside units (RSUs). A trust evaluation framework has been accordingly established, wherein other vehicles have been exploited for evaluating the vehicles requesting the content and the RSUs during the content delivery process. A bargaining game theoretic pricing model has been further envisaged with an intent to facilitate both the vehicles and the RSUs to interact more positively for improving their respective trust scores. With significantly higher trust scores, the vehicles are capable of minimizing the cost of the accessed services and the RSUs are, in turn, able to earn higher profits by attracting more vehicles. Finally, the envisaged framework has been analyzed in (a) a two-round game and (b) an M-round game for realizing the secure delivery of content and to optimize the utilities of players (the vehicles and the RSUs).

In [26], a trust-aware communication architecture for social IoV has been proposed that takes into consideration the humans and a vehicle's location-based honesty for ascertaining a vehicle's and, its driver's and the passengers' trust. The honesty factor of both the driver and the passengers is ascertained by taking into consideration their online social networking profiles. Furthermore, the current location of the vehicles is also compared vis-à-vis their respective estimated location, based on their past/historical mobility patterns, in order to ascertain the similarity measurement. In [27], a fuzzy logic-based decentralized trust evaluation has been envisaged for vehicular Internet of things in order to ascertain the direct trust once a trustee is within the transmission range of a trustor. The referred approach takes into consideration the notions of cooperativeness (measured as the number of successful forwarding jobs carried out by a trustee), honestness (ascertained via the number of honest packets sent by a trustee), and responsibility (assessed as the percentage of events that are detected by a trustee to the ones reported by a trustee). A Q-learning, i.e., reinforcement learning, algorithm has been further employed to ascertain the indirect trust of a node via its one-hop neighbors especially if a trustee's behavior cannot be observed directly.

In [28], a hybrid trust mechanism and an MDS have been proposed, wherein a trust metric is assigned to all of the vehicles primarily depending on their respective behavior. Accordingly, a vehicle with the highest trustworthy score is elected as the group leader which, in turn, interacts with the other group members and the back-end system so as to ascertain a malicious vehicle. The malicious vehicle is subsequently reported to the misbehavior authority which is, in fact, responsible for limiting its consequences via appropriate actions. In [29], a global roaming trust-based model has been suggested in an attempt to handle internal attacks during V2X communication, wherein trust is maintained at both the road level and the RSU level. The road entities are not only tasked for ascertaining the trustworthiness of other entities in their immediate ambience but to also disseminate the necessary warnings to the nearby RSUs on the identification of the malicious entity. The RSUs, in turn, inform the same to the central server which makes the ultimate decision before broadcasting the global blacklist back to the RSUs. The model has been evaluated under a selective forwarding attack and a recommendation attack. In [30], a distributed reputation management system (DREAMS) has been envisaged for both the identification and elimination of malicious vehicles. Each vehicle ascertains the trust of its one-hop neighbors, and accordingly, forwards the same to its corresponding local authority which then weighs and subsequently aggregates them to update and exhibit the reputation values of respective vehicles. These reputation values are accordingly stored in a global reputation database. When a vehicle traverses into a new region, the local vehicles (along with the service providers) can query its reputation score before initiating any sort of interaction.

In contrast to the above referred trust-based research studies, our envisaged trust model intelligently weighs the reputation segments, both direct and indirect, by taking into consideration the dynamic context of each observing vehicle in terms of its overtime acquaintance with a trustee, the degree of similar content accessed by a trustor and a trustee, and relevance of the reputation segments with respect to their timeliness. Furthermore, instead of enforcing a fixed trustworthiness threshold, our trust model also introduces an inspection threshold, along with an allocation of additional time to vehicles under certain specific conditions, in order to ensure that only misbehaving vehicles are eliminated from an IoV network and the ones that have been bad-mouthed are reintegrated in an appropriate manner.

3.3 Trust Management – Preliminaries

In this section, we discuss the fundamentals of the promising paradigm of trust, i.e., its qualitative and quantitative forms of measurement and its subjective and objective nature, together with a brief illustration of some of the malicious attacks that could be launched on trust management systems.

3.3.1 Trust as a Paradigm

Trust is a multi-faceted paradigm and has thus been employed in a diverse range of domains. Its foundations are strongly rooted in the human society, wherein it is used as a psychological measurement in assisting a human or an object, i.e., trustor, to firm up its decision of interacting with the other humans or objects, i.e., trustees. The outcome of such an interaction transpires in either the trustor in realizing its certain objectives or the trustor getting harmed by a trustee in an unfortunate event of a misplaced trust. Although trust has been delineated by researchers in both academia and industry in a number of ways, in its simplest form, trust is generally referred to as the confidence of one human (or an object) over the other [31, 32, 33]. In other words, it manifests the degree of a belief or a disbelief of one human (or an object) over the other for executing a specific task or a set of tasks in an anticipated manner. We, accordingly, define *trust* as follows:

"Trust could be either categorized as a qualitative or a quantitative property of a trustee which is ascertained by a trustor in a subjective or an objective manner for a certain task within a specific context at any given period of time".

Here, the terminology of a trustor has been employed to refer to an object that takes some sort of an initiative of interacting with another object and a trustee as an object with whom the interactions have been carried out for obtaining the necessary information. The nature of the measurement could be either quantitative or qualitative. The quantitative forms of measurement of trust include, but are not limited to, (a) similarity – the degree of similar content and/or services accessed by both a trustor and a trustee, (b) familiarity – how well a trustor is acquainted with a trustee, (c) packet delivery ratio – the throughput between a trustor and a trustee, and (d) accuracy – how much trustworthy is a particular node or what is the optimum threshold for ascertaining if a node is categorized as a trustworthy or an untrustworthy one. Similarly, the qualitative forms of measurement of trust encompasses (a) motivation – a psychological state which manifests a trustor's desire for building and subsequently maintaining a trustworthy relationship with a trustee, (b) awareness – the knowledge or perception of a trustor pertinent to a specific context and any dynamic changes that transpire therein, and (c) commitment – a mediating factor that influences the relationship durability between a trustor and a trustee since a strong commitment facilitates in stabilizing a relationship and is ensured if a trustor's needs are continuously met as a result of its interactions with a trustee.

Furthermore, trust could be either subjective or objective in its nature, i.e., a subjective trust is ascertained as a consequence of a direct interaction with a trustee, whereas, on the contrary, an objective trust of a trustee is ascertained by obtaining the subjective trust of its peers (i.e., immediate neighbors). Finally, it is indispensable to ascertain the trust for a particular task within a specific context at any given period of time. For instance, a node might trust another node in order to realize (a) a particular objective, i.e., task-dependent trust, (b) for a certain duration of time and not on a persistent basis, i.e., time-dependent trust, and (c) in a particular context, i.e., a node might trust another node in one context and not in a different context, i.e., context-dependent trust [13, 30]. We define a *trust model* as follows:

*"A trust model comprises of a weighted amalgamation of direct trust and
indirect trust representing the overall trustworthiness of a trustee. These
weights are ascertained on the basis of a number of different quality
attributes, i.e., primarily dependent on the context, and with potential of
influencing the trustworthiness of a trustee".*

Trust models could be segregated into three types, i.e., data-oriented trust
models, entity-oriented trust models, and hybrid trust models. In case of the
data-oriented trust models, data plays an indispensable role and the trust is
ascertained by evaluating the accuracy and authenticity of the received messages rather than evaluating the trust of a message sender. On the contrary,
the entity-oriented trust models ascertain the trust of a node to identify, and
accordingly, eliminate misbehaving nodes from a network. Finally, the hybrid
trust models aggregate the salient features pertinent to both the data-oriented
and the entity-oriented trust models for the purposes of trust management
[22, 34].

3.3.2   Attacks on Trust Management Systems

There are numerous sorts of attacks which can affect the trustworthiness of
a vehicle subsequently impacting its authenticity within the network, including but not limited to, opportunistic service attacks, self-promoting attacks,
on-off attacks, selective behavior attacks, bad-mouthing attacks, and ballot
stuffing attacks. The opportunistic service attacks, self-promoting attacks, on-
off attacks, and selective behavior attacks are the common forms of attacks
primarily based on self-interest, whereas, the bad-mouthing and ballot stuffing attacks represent the class of reputation-based attacks [35, 36, 37]. These
attacks are illustrated as follows:

- *Opportunistic Service Attack* – In case of an opportunistic service attack,
  a misbehaving vehicle primarily acts in a disguise, i.e., honest mode, and
  initiates malign activities once it finds itself in an optimal position to do
  so. In other words, a malicious vehicle furnishes a better service in a bid to
  obtain a higher reputation in an IoV network, and once the same has been
  established, it starts acting opportunistically and furnishes bad service. It
  is also pertinent to note that, vehicles as part of a vehicular networking environment, interact with one another for realizing a number of cooperative
  vehicular safety and non-safety applications and services. Hence, misbehaving vehicles possessing good reputation can effectively collude with the other
  misbehaving vehicles so as to launch various sophisticated attacks such as
  the bad-mouthing attack and the ballot stuffing attack [38].

- *Self-promoting Attack* – In the context of a self-promoting attack, a misbehaving vehicle constantly augments its reputation in a bid to acquire significant privileges within an IoV network so that it is able to jeopardize the
  same for its malign gains [39, 40]. In order to realize such sort of an attack,

a misbehaving vehicle can generate sophisticated Sybil, i.e., pseudonymous, identities to enhance its trust, thereby misleading the traditional reputation mechanisms [41].

- *On-off Attack* – In an on-off attack, a misbehaving vehicle randomly operates between a good and a bad behavior to maintain an appropriate reputation within an IoV network in an attempt to ensure that its chances of acquiring privileges remain considerably higher. Hence, by providing a good and a bad reputation in a zig-zag manner, the probability of a misbehaving vehicle for being classified as malicious with low reputation value ultimately evades [42, 43, 44, 45].

- *Selective Behavior Attack* – In a selective behavior attack, a misbehaving vehicle performs good for one particular set of services and bad for the other set of services. For instance, a misbehaving vehicle may act good for services that are characterized as requiring low computational requirements. This thus allows misbehaving vehicles to preserve resources by facilitating less demanding services in an IoV network. This sort of a behavior is considered as malicious since vehicles in a collaborative network work in a cooperative manner to allow the network to operate effectively. Nevertheless, in this manner, i.e., wherein a malicious vehicle does not deliberately cater for the computational intensive services, it is still able to maintain its reasonable reputation in an IoV network [46, 47].

- *Bad-mouthing Attack* – In a bad-mouthing attack, a misbehaving vehicle harms the reputation of an honest vehicle by providing bad recommendations on the same. This, therefore, hampers the probability of a honest vehicle for gaining any significant privileges in an IoV network. Bad-mouthing attack generally transpires in the form of a group, wherein a number of misbehaving vehicles collude together in order to diminish the trust of a particular honest vehicle [43, 48].

- *Ballot Stuffing Attack* – In an IoV network, the misbehaving vehicles can also come together to augment the trust score of a particular vehicle possessing malicious intentions which, in turn, increases its chances of gaining significant privileges in an IoV network. This sort of an attack is generally referred to as the ballot stuffing attack. Should a malicious vehicle ends up getting elected as a cluster head, this could have dire consequences for both the security and reliability of an IoV network, thereby proving fatal for both the vehicular passengers and the vulnerable pedestrians [13].

3.4   The System Model

We, hereby, envisage an IoV network encompassing trusted and misbehaving vehicles (herein referred to as nodes) $V_i, i = \{1, \ldots, I\}$. The trust values

$T_{V_i,V_j,t}; 1 \leq j \leq I; j \neq i$ are allocated to each of the node V_i by its N_i one-hop neighboring nodes ($N_i = \{V_j \mid V_j \in \{V_1, V_2, ..., V_I\}\}$ and $n_i = \{V_{j'}\}$, wherein $j' \in j$ is a subset of the nodes without the trustor) at every time instance $t = \{1, ..., t_o\}$. The trust values are ascertained and subsequently allocated on the basis of a node's behavior, i.e., the nodes disseminating legitimate information are considered as trusted, and accordingly, are assigned a higher trust value. On the contrary, the nodes disseminating malicious information are categorized as untrusted and trust values, in turn, assigned to them are considerably low. Trust values vary in the range of *0* and *1*, wherein *0* implies an untrusted node at any time instance t, whereas, *1* signifies the highest level of trust. Therefore, the total trust for a vehicle V_i ascertained by a vehicle V_j is computed as:

$$T_{(V_i,V_j,t)}^{\text{Total}} = \alpha_{(V_i,V_j,t)} \cdot T_{(V_i,V_j,t)}^{\text{Direct}} + (1 - \alpha_{(V_i,V_j,t)}) \cdot T_{(V_i,V_j,t)}^{\text{Indirect}}, \qquad (3.1)$$

where, $\alpha_{(V_i,V_j,t)}$ and $(1 - \alpha_{(V_i,V_j,t)})$ refer to the weights of the direct trust and the indirect trust, respectively.

The mathematical notations employed in the envisaged IoV-based trust computational model are depicted in Table 3.1.

3.4.1 Direct Trust

The direct trust, $0 \leq T^{\text{Direct}} \leq 1$, within an IoV network is referred to as a trustor's (one-hop neighboring vehicle's) direct observation of a trustee and is ascertained as:

$$T_{(V_i,V_j,t)}^{\text{Direct}} = \beta \cdot T_{(V_i,V_j,t_o)} + (1 - \beta) \cdot T_{(V_i,V_j,t_{o-1})}, \qquad (3.2)$$

wherein, t_o refers to the tth interaction of a trustor with a trustee, i.e., interaction at the current time instance, for ascertaining the trust and t_{o-1} manifests the trust ascertained by a trustor at an earlier time instance. Herein, β is a smoothing update factor and thus varies in the range of $0.5 \leq \beta \leq 1$. This demonstrates that we are not merely overwriting the previous trust values, rather, we are employing a smoothing update procedure [28] in order to ensure that the impact of the earlier trust segments is also taken into consideration, i.e., to some extent. Furthermore, the range of β has been adjusted since we are quite more interested in the recent trust segments in contrast to the earlier trust segments.

For the sake of the readers' clarity, a trust segment is generally referred to as any interaction between a trustor and a trustee. Furthermore, it is indispensable to highlight that the value of β is also dependent on a particular context and is either set by the system designers, or alternatively, the system should be intelligent enough so as to ascertain the prevalent context in order to opt for an appropriate smoothing update factor.

3.4.2 Indirect Trust

The indirect trust, $0 \leq T^{\text{Indirect}} \leq 1$, generally referred to as the recommendation (or reputation), facilitates in ascertaining the trustworthiness of a trustee depending on the opinion(s) of a trusted third party or a network of trusted third parties. The indirect trust is computed as:

$$T^{\text{Indirect}}_{(V_i,V_j,t)} = \frac{1}{|n_i|} \cdot \sum_{V_{j'} \in n_i} T^{\text{Direct}}_{(V_i,V_{j'},t)}, \tag{3.3}$$

wherein, n_i manifests the number of remaining one-hop neighboring vehicles of a targeted vehicle and $T^{\text{Direct}}_{(V_i,V_{j'},t)}$ refers to the direct trust ascertained by each of these remaining neighboring vehicles. This manifests that the indirect trust of a vehicle V_i is the mean of the direct trusts ascertained by j' vehicles in the V_i's neighborhood. We have employed the arithmetic mean here as it is highly relevant when numerous quantities are accumulated together especially if they are not reliant on one another [49].

The notions of the direct and the indirect trust are depicted in Figure 3.1. Moreover, the aggregated trust for a vehicle V_i at a single time instance is determined as:

$$T^{\text{Aggregate}}_{(V_i,V_j,t)} = \frac{1}{|N_i|} \cdot \sum_{V_j \in N_i} T^{\text{Total}}_{(V_i,V_j,t)}, \tag{3.4}$$

here, N_i refers to the total number of vehicles that have interacted, and accordingly, allocated the trust to a vehicle V_i.

3.4.3   Weight Computation

Subsequent to ascertaining of both the direct and the indirect trust, the next step is to amalgamate them together in order to formulate a final trust score. Nevertheless, this amalgamation is primarily reliant on their respective weights which themselves need to be computed in an appropriate manner. These weights take into consideration three salient quality attributes, i.e., familiarity, similarity, and timeliness, which have the potential to impact the overall trustworthiness of a trustee. These trust attributes are illustrated as follows:

- *Familiarity*: The notion of familiarity facilitates in ascertaining how well a one-hop neighbor is acquainted with that of a targeted vehicle. If the familiarity of any trust segment is high, this implies that a trustor has more prior knowledge pertinent to a trustee and is in a better position of making informed decisions. Therefore, reputation segments possessing higher familiarity are indispensable in ascertaining a reliable trust computation,

- *Similarity*: Similarity refers to the degree of similar content (i.e., vehicular applications and services and the data involved therein) accessed by a trustor and a trustee, and

- *Timeliness*: Timeliness delineates on the freshness of any reputation segment, i.e., how fresh is a neighbor's opinion pertinent to a targeted vehicle.

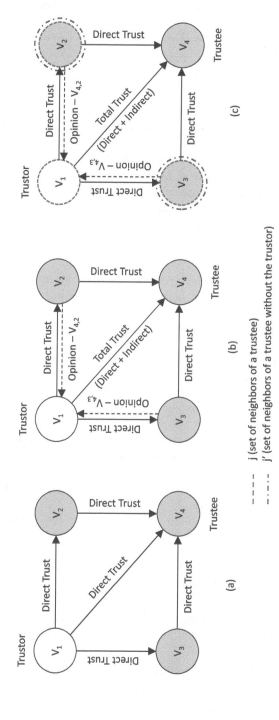

FIGURE 3.1

Depicting a pairwise trust-based relationship: (a) portrays direct trust, (b) highlights indirect trust, i.e., in the form of opinions (recommendations), in addition to the direct trust, and (c) illustrates the set of neighbors of a trustee (with and without a trustor).

TABLE 3.1

Mathematical notations employed in the envisaged IoV-based trust computational model.

Notation	Description
$T^{\text{Total}}_{(V_i,V_j,t)}$	Total trust ascertained for a vehicle V_i by a vehicle V_j at a time instance t.
$T^{\text{Direct}}_{(V_i,V_j,t)}$	Direct trust ascertained for a vehicle V_i by a vehicle V_j at a time instance t.
$T_{(V_i,V_j,t_o)}$	Direct trust ascertained for a vehicle V_i by a vehicle V_j at the current time instance, i.e., t_o.
$T_{(V_i,V_j,t_{o-1})}$	Direct trust ascertained for a vehicle V_i by a vehicle V_j at an earlier time instance, i.e., t_{o-1}.
$T^{\text{Indirect}}_{(V_i,V_j,t)}$	Recommendations (opinions) of a trusted third party or a network of trusted third parties pertinent to a trustee.
$T^{\text{Aggregate}}_{(V_i,V_j,t)}$	Aggregate trust for a vehicle V_i at a time instant t.
$\alpha_{(V_i,V_j,t)}$	Weightage of the direct trust ($T^{\text{Direct}}_{(V_i,V_j,t)}$).
$1 - \alpha_{(V_i,V_j,t)}$	Weightage of the indirect trust ($T^{\text{Indirect}}_{(V_i,V_j,t)}$).
β	Smoothing update factor to ensure that the impact of the earlier trust segments between a vehicle V_i and a vehicle V_j is taken into consideration to some extent.
$fm_{(V_i,V_j,t)}$	Familiarity or the acquaintance of a vehicle V_j (trustor, i.e., one-hop neighbor) with that of a vehicle V_i (trustee).
$b_{(V_i,V_j,t)}$	Belief on a vehicle V_i by a vehicle V_j
$d_{(V_i,V_j,t)}$	Disbelief on a vehicle V_i by a vehicle V_j
$u_{(V_i,V_j,t)}$	Uncertainty of a vehicle V_j in a vehicle V_i
$sm_{(V_i,V_j,t)}$	Degree of similar content accessed by a vehicle V_i and a vehicle V_j
$tm_{(V_i,V_j,t)}$	A measure of delay between the current time instance and time when the opinion about a vehicle V_i was formed by a vehicle V_j.
$T^{\text{Threshold}}$	A trust threshold selected to classify/segregate honest and misbehaving vehicles.
$T^{\text{Inspection}}$	An inspection threshold to ensure that the vehicle being inspected is in fact a misbehaving one ($T^{\text{Aggregate}} < T^{\text{Inspection}}$).
$t_{inspection}$	Time for which a vehicle with decaying trust needs to be inspected against the respective thresholds.

Hence, by taking into consideration the notion of familiarity, similarity, and timeliness, the requisite weight, i.e., $\alpha_{(V_i,V_j,t)}$, of any reputation segment is calculated as:

$$\alpha_{(V_i,V_j,t)} = fm_{(V_i,V_j,t)} + sm_{(V_i,V_j,t)} + tm_{(V_i,V_j,t)}. \tag{3.5}$$

In the sequel, we will illustrate one-by-one as to how these three trust attributes are ascertained in our IoV-based trust model.

3.4.3.1 Familiarity

Familiarity is computed via subjective logic that applies opinions for representing the subjective belief [50]. These opinions take into consideration the degree of trust (belief $- b_{(V_i,V_j,t)}$) and the distrust (disbelief $- d_{(V_i,V_j,t)}$) on a vehicle V_i by a vehicle V_j, vehicle V_j's uncertainty ($u_{(V_i,V_j,t)}$) in a vehicle V_i – a measure of the confidence of a vehicle V_j's knowledge on a vehicle V_i, and a base rate ($r_{(V_i,V_j,t)}$) which is a pre-defined constant and represents the willingness of a vehicle V_j to believe in a vehicle V_i. Both belief and disbelief are dependent on a vehicle's benign and malicious behaviors, respectively. Similar to the research work envisaged in [30, 50], a tuple ($b_{(V_i,V_j,t)}, d_{(V_i,V_j,t)}, u_{(V_i,V_j,t)}, r_{(V_i,V_j,t)}$) has been employed for expressing the subjective logic. Hence, the expectation of a vehicle V_j that a vehicle V_i would act cooperatively, i.e., vehicle V_j's expectation of a vehicle V_i acting quite rationally, is depicted as:

$$expectation_{(V_i,V_j,t)} = b_{(V_i,V_j,t)} + u_{(V_i,V_j,t)} \cdot r_{(V_i,V_j,t)}. \tag{3.6}$$

Hence, if an opinion is (0.79, 0.11, 0.10, 0.50), its expectation becomes $expectation_{(V_i,V_j,t)} = b_{(V_i,V_j,t)} + u_{(V_i,V_j,t)} \cdot r_{(V_i,V_j,t)} = (0.79) + (0.10) \times (0.50) = 0.84$. On the contrary, an absolutely uncertain opinion of (0.0, 0.0, 1.0, $r_{(V_i,V_j,t)}$) reflects an expectation equivalent to the base rate, i.e., $expectation_{(V_i,V_j,t)} = (0.0) + (1.0) \times r_{(V_i,V_j,t)} = r_{(V_i,V_j,t)}$. The relationship between $b_{(V_i,V_j,t)}$, $d_{(V_i,V_j,t)}$, and $u_{(V_i,V_j,t)}$ is given as:

$$b_{(V_i,V_j,t)} + d_{(V_i,V_j,t)} + u_{(V_i,V_j,t)} = 1, \tag{3.7}$$

and, familiarity ($fm_{(V_i,V_j,t)}$) being a sum of belief and disbelief is computed as:

$$fm_{(V_i,V_j,t)} = b_{(V_i,V_j,t)} + d_{(V_i,V_j,t)} = 1 - u_{(V_i,V_j,t)}. \tag{3.8}$$

For binary events, either satisfactory or unsatisfactory, the notions of belief, disbelief, and uncertainty could be computed as:

$$b_{V_i,V_j,t} = \frac{\sum_{t=1}^{t_o} s_{(V_i,V_j,t)}}{\sum_{t=1}^{t_o} s_{(V_i,V_j,t)} + \sum_{t=1}^{t_o} us_{(V_i,V_j,t)} + 2}, \tag{3.9}$$

$$d_{V_i,V_j,t} = \frac{\sum_{t=1}^{t_o} us_{(V_i,V_j,t)}}{\sum_{t=1}^{t_o} s_{(V_i,V_j,t)} + \sum_{t=1}^{t_o} us_{(V_i,V_j,t)} + 2}, \tag{3.10}$$

$$u_{V_i,V_j,t} = \frac{2}{\sum_{t=1}^{t_o} s_{(V_i,V_j,t)} + \sum_{t=1}^{t_o} us_{(V_i,V_j,t)} + 2}, \tag{3.11}$$

here, $s_{(V_i,V_j,t)}$ and $us_{(V_i,V_j,t)}$ refer to the satisfactory and the unsatisfactory trust segments between a trustor and a trustee, respectively. It is pertinent to mention that this is much different to what has been suggested in [30] since the later takes into consideration a synthetic reputation segment, i.e., formed by a local authority as a result of the weighted average of all the reputation segments pertinent to a trustee, in order to ascertain the notions of belief, disbelief, and uncertainty (also referred, therein, as the parameters of the synthetic reputation segment). These notions are subsequently updated, i.e., a new opinion is formed, by combining via a subjective logic consensus operation, the synthetic reputation segment and the last reputation value of the trustee (historical knowledge) obtained from the local or the global reputation database depending on whether the local authority has previously interacted with the trustee or not. In essence, [30] employs the subjective logic for the reputation update of a trustee, whereas, our research employs the subjective logic to ascertain the familiarity between a trustor and a trustee by particularly taking into account their satisfactory and unsatisfactory interactions. Next, we would provide the justification for Equations (3.9), (3.10), and (3.11).

Justification [51, 52]

The posterior probability pertinent to the binary events, i.e., for the scenarios, wherein the relative atomicity of an actual trust-based event in an IoV network turns out to be $\frac{1}{2}$, can be represented via the beta distribution. The beta distribution, in essence, signifies the probability distribution of probabilities and models continuous random variables parameterized in terms of α and β. The probability density function of the beta distribution, for $0 \leq p \leq 1$ and $\alpha, \beta > 0$, is ascertained as:

$$f(p|\alpha,\beta) = \frac{1}{B(\alpha+\beta)} \cdot p^{\alpha-1} \cdot (1-p)^{\beta-1}, \tag{3.12}$$

where, $B(\alpha,\beta)$ is the beta function and can be expressed in terms of the gamma (Γ) function, i.e., $B(\alpha,\beta) = \frac{\Gamma(\alpha)\cdot\Gamma(\beta)}{\Gamma(\alpha+\beta)}$. Equation (3.12) can, therefore, be rewritten as:

$$f(p|\alpha,\beta) = \frac{\Gamma(\alpha+\beta)}{\Gamma(\alpha)\cdot\Gamma(\beta)} \cdot p^{\alpha-1} \cdot (1-p)^{\beta-1}, \tag{3.13}$$

with the constraint that $p \neq 0$ if $\alpha < 1$ and $p \neq 1$ if $\beta < 1$. Moreover, the expectation of the beta distribution is expressed as:

$$E(p) = \frac{\alpha}{\alpha+\beta}. \tag{3.14}$$

Furthermore, since we have to account for the event spaces of arbitrary atomicity, hence, the trust-based events of arbitrary relative atomicity can be ascertained as:

$$\begin{aligned} \alpha &= s + 2r, & s \geq 0, 0 < r < 1 \\ \beta &= us + 2(1-r), & us \geq 0, 0 < r < 1 \end{aligned} \tag{3.15}$$

here, r refers to the relative atomicity of a trust-based actual event, and s and us manifest the evidence supporting and negating the said event, i.e., positive and negative evidence, respectively. Hence, Equation (3.14), subsequent to the incorporation of α and β from Equation (3.15), can be rewritten as:

$$E(p) = \frac{s + 2r}{s + us + 2}. \tag{3.16}$$

By equating the expectation values delineated in Equation (3.6) and Equation (3.16) and by employing Equation (3.7), we obtain the following:

$$\begin{cases} b + u \cdot r = \dfrac{s + 2r}{s + us + 2}, \\ b + d + u = 1, \end{cases} \implies \begin{cases} b + u \cdot r = \dfrac{s}{s + us + 2} + \dfrac{2r}{s + us + 2}, \\ b + d + u = 1. \end{cases} \tag{3.17}$$

In order to ensure affinity between belief (b) and positive evidence (s) and disbelief (d) and negative evidence (us), we desire b and d to be the increasing functions of s and us, respectively. We further require uncertainty (u) to be a decreasing function of (s, us). Taking into account these affinity requirements, we can derive the following from Equation (3.17):

$$\begin{cases} b = \dfrac{s}{s + us + 2}, \\ d = \dfrac{us}{s + us + 2}, \\ u = \dfrac{2}{s + us + 2}. \end{cases} \tag{3.18}$$

3.4.3.2 Similarity

Similarity is yet another indispensable factor and relates to the degree of the similar content (i.e., vehicular applications and services and the data involved therein) accessed by any two vehicles. If a vehicle V_i has more content similarity with that of a vehicle V_j, the corresponding opinion would be of relatively higher reliability. Therefore, the content similarity among the two vehicles V_i and V_j is ascertained as:

$$s_{(V_i, V_j, t)} = |C_{V_i, t} \cap C_{V_j, t}|, \tag{3.19}$$

wherein, C_{v_i} and C_{v_j} refers to the content accessed at a time instance t by the vehicles V_i and V_j, respectively.

3.4.3.3 Timeliness

Timeliness refers to the freshness of a neighbor's opinion pertinent to a targeted vehicle and is manifested via the power law distribution [30]:

$$tm_{(V_i, V_j, t)} = \eta_{sc}(t_o - t_{(V_i, V_j)})^{-\varepsilon}, \tag{3.20}$$

here, $t_o - t_{(V_i, V_j)}$ refers to a delay between the current time instance t_o and the time $t_{(V_i, V_j)}$, i.e., when an opinion about a vehicle V_i was formed by a vehicle V_j. In a highly dynamic vehicular networking environment, timeliness plays an extremely crucial role since vehicles frequently interact with one another and keeps on updating their opinions based on their own dynamic context and the dynamic context of a targeted vehicle. Moreover, the power law here delineates an inverse relationship between the time delay and the timeliness. η_{sc} here is a pre-defined scaling constant, whereas, ε is the power law's exponent.

3.4.4 Trust Threshold

Once the requisite weights have been ascertained and trust has been appropriately computed, it is indispensable to determine if a particular vehicle is trustworthy or untrustworthy at any particular time instance and at any of the subsequent time instances. Therefore, a trustworthy threshold, $T^{\text{Threshold}}$, needs to be selected in order to guarantee that any misbehaving vehicle could be appropriately eliminated from an IoV network. Nevertheless, vehicles should not be instantly removed once their respective trust scores fall below the selected threshold since even a honest vehicle might experience a low trust score for a small duration of time in case it avoids frequent network participation with an intent to avoid the battery failure. Accordingly, in our envisaged IoV-based trust model, once the trust value of a certain vehicle falls below the selected threshold, $T^{\text{Aggregate}} < T^{\text{Threshold}}$, the said vehicle enters in an inspection phase for a particular period of time, $t_{inspection}$, and is therefore investigated against an inspection threshold, $T^{\text{Inspection}}$. Furthermore, if the trust of a vehicle being inspected falls below the inspection threshold, $T^{\text{Aggregate}} < T^{\text{Inspection}}$, it would be considered as a misbehaving vehicle and is instantaneously removed from an IoV network.

Similarly, if the trust of a vehicle under inspection ranges in between the selected threshold and an inspection threshold, $T^{\text{Inspection}} < T^{\text{Aggregate}} < T^{\text{Threshold}}$, and does not (a) exceed the selected threshold, $T^{\text{Aggregate}} > T^{\text{Threshold}}$, or (b) demonstrate any sort of improvement within its trust score during the inspection period, it would still be categorized as a misbehaving vehicle and is subsequently removed from an IoV network. However, under the same conditions, if a vehicle demonstrates some sort of an improvement in its trust score, it would be allocated an additional period of time (i.e., equivalent to the original inspection period) in order to observe if it could be reintegrated back into the network. Consequent to this, if the trust of a vehicle under inspection exceeds the trustworthy threshold, $T^{\text{Aggregate}} > T^{\text{Threshold}}$, then that particular vehicle would be categorized as an honest one and is reintegrated back into an IoV network. These particular sets of rules are illustrated in Figure 3.2.

3.5 Experimental Settings and Results

In this section, we describe the experimental setup and report the experimental results for our envisaged IoV-based trust computational model. An IoV

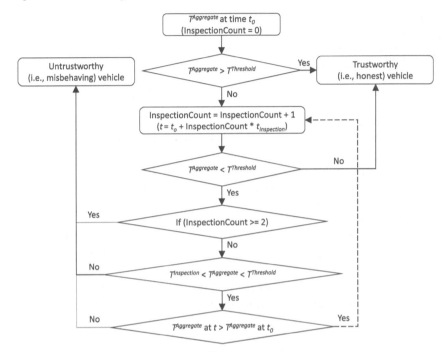

FIGURE 3.2
An illustration of trustworthiness evaluation rules for identifying trustworthy (honest) and untrustworthy (misbehaving) vehicles in an IoV network.

simulator has been programmed in Java and the traces obtained in the form of a data set have been subsequently investigated in MATLAB. The simulation area encompasses vehicles with diverse speeds which randomly traverse along a set of diverse paths throughout the network and simultaneously interact with the other vehicles within an IoV network. This interaction time primarily depends on the speed of a trustor and a trustee. The speed of all the vehicles remains uniform during their trajectory along a single path and alters only once a new path has been selected by a respective vehicle. Since vehicles interact to realize a number of safety-critical and non-safety infotainment applications, the direct trust is, therefore, ascertained by taking into account the ratio of the number of successful interactions to the total interactions between a trustor and a trustee. This way of ascertaining the direct trust is perhaps one of the most logical and acceptable mechanisms in the research literature [6, 15, 53, 54]. Also, malicious vehicles have been injected into the IoV network which possess the capability to instigate a bad-mouthing (slandering) as well as a self-promoting attack. In order to simulate the bad-mouthing attack, a collusion-based strategy has been introduced, wherein the malicious vehicles act in tandem to assign bad reputation to the honest vehicles in a purely randomized manner. Please note that a randomized strategy has been adopted

TABLE 3.2

Simulation parameters.

Parameters	Value
Simulation area	600 x 600
Simulation time	30 minutes
No. of simulated iterations	5
Speed of the vehicles	Variable
Weight of the direct $(\alpha_{(V_i, V_j, t)})$ and the indirect trust $(1 - \alpha_{(V_i, V_j, t)})$	Derived (Section 3.4.3)
Smoothing update factor (β)	R: $[0.5, 1]$
Pre-defined scaling constant (η_{sc})	10
Power law's exponent (ε)	1.05
Trust threshold $(T^{\text{Threshold}})$	0.5
Inspection threshold $(T^{\text{Inspection}})$	0.4
Inspection time $(t_{inspection})$	10 seconds (each)

to bring the simulations as close to the reality as possible. On the contrary, the self-promoting attack has been simulated by providing the misbehaving vehicles with a provision to fabricate a positive feedback for themselves.

It is pertinent to highlight here that our IoV Simulator is also based on the principles of an open source traffic simulator, i.e., Simulation of Urban Mobility (SUMO)[2]. However, the reason for designing a purpose-built IoV simulator and not using SUMO is that the latter, on its own, does not offer the provision for simulating the notion of trust, various trust attributes, and intricate trust-related attacks, and instead relies on the external, i.e., third-party, applications to do so. In other words, SUMO generates the mobility traces of the road traffic, whereas, the third party applications govern and employ the same. On the contrary, the IoV simulator envisaged for our research is particularly designed with trust management in mind so that the salient characteristics of trust are not only well-integrated but can be extensively tested too. Furthermore, the real challenge here is not the complexity of the road traffic but the social interactions amongst the vehicles and is, therefore, facilitated by our IoV simulator. It is also noteworthy to mention that experiments carried out on similar IoV Simulators has already been acknowledged in the research literature [35]. The simulation parameters employed in our experiments are delineated in Table 3.2.

Figure 3.3 portrays the trust values of randomly selected six misbehaving vehicles in an IoV network subsequent to an observing time duration of 30 minutes. It is also pertinent to highlight that the misbehaving vehicles either act in a selfish manner or even possess a malicious behavior such as the intentional dropping of relaying packets. Hence, the trust values assigned to the misbehaving vehicles via our envisaged IoV-based trust model have been compared vis-á-vis the ones ascertained via the state-of-the-art trust models

---

[2]https://www.eclipse.org/sumo/.

proposed in [28] and [29] (hereafter referred to as the baseline models). It is apparent that the trust values assigned to the misbehaving vehicles via our envisaged model are comparatively lower in contrast to the ones assigned by the referred baseline models. The underlying rationale for the same lies in an intelligent weights' assignment for both the direct and the indirect trust, which takes into consideration the quality attributes of familiarity, content similarity, and timeliness. In this manner, we are capable of paying a much closer attention to the reputation segments with higher qualities in contrast to the ones possessing lower qualities. This, in tandem with an intelligent trust threshold mechanism, facilitates in an earlier elimination of the misbehaving vehicles from an IoV network.

Furthermore, for the demonstration purposes, we have randomly selected a misbehaving vehicle and portrayed its trust values over the simulated time duration via our envisaged IoV-based trust model and the baseline models in Figure 3.4(a). It could be easily observed that the trust of the misbehaving vehicle via our envisaged trust model deteriorates rapidly over the time in contrast to the two referred baseline models, i.e., the misbehaving vehicle traversed into the IoV network at time $t = 6^{th}$ minute and was hence marked and accordingly eliminated from the network towards the end of time $t = 13^{th}$ minute subsequent to its due inspection periods. On the contrary, the baseline models were unable to identify the misbehaving vehicle, i.e., primarily owing to its selfish or malicious behavior, consequently resulting in deterioration of the entire network. The conduct of the said vehicle in its last minute is also depicted in Figure 3.4(b).

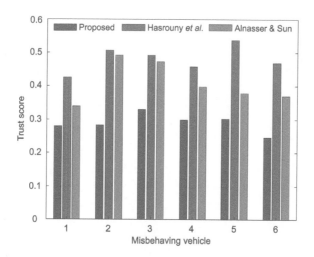

FIGURE 3.3
Comparison of the trust scores of six misbehaving vehicles via our envisaged IoV-based trust model vis-á-vis the baseline models, i.e., Hasrouny et al. [28] and Alnasser & Sun [29], in an IoV network subsequent to an observing time window of 30 minutes.

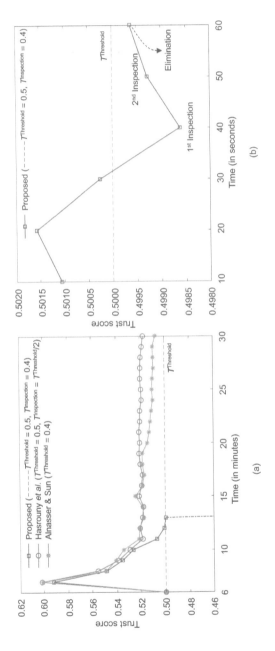

FIGURE 3.4

(a) Trust values of a misbehaving vehicle over the simulated time duration (i.e., of 30 minutes) via our envisaged IoV-based trust model vis-á-vis the baseline models, i.e., Hasrouny et al. [28] and Alnasser & Sun [29], (b) Conduct of the misbehaving vehicle during its last 60 seconds of stay in an IoV network as per the envisaged IoV-based trust model.

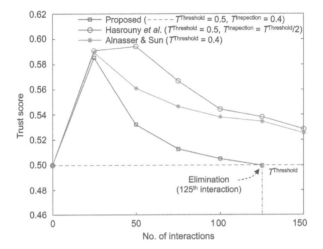

FIGURE 3.5
Number of interactions encountered by a misbehaving vehicle via our envisaged IoV-based trust model vis-á-vis the baseline models, i.e., Hasrouny et al.
[28] and Alnasser & Sun [29].

Figure 3.5 further depicts the change in the trust values of a misbehaving vehicle via our envisaged IoV-based trust model and the referred baseline
models vis-á-vis the number of interactions it had encountered with the other
vehicles in its immediate ambience within an IoV network. These include interactions with the similar as well as different vehicles (traversing with varying
speeds and directions) along the course of its traveling trajectory. It could be,
therefore, observed that our envisaged IoV-based trust model identified and
subsequently eliminated the misbehaving vehicle even if it had encountered
fewer interactions in contrast to the considerable number of interactions encountered via the other two baseline models. As a *single* misbehaving vehicle
can cause a menace, our envisaged IoV-based trust model ensures a timely
elimination of such vehicles. This is of much essence since fewer interactions
not only facilitate in conserving the resources of the interacting vehicles but
also mitigates the network management overhead.

Furthermore, Figure 3.6(a) manifests the average percentage of misbehaving vehicles correctly identified by our envisaged IoV-based trust model vis-
á-vis the referred baseline models over the simulated time duration. It could
be observed that the average percentage of misbehaving vehicles identified by
our envisaged IoV-based trust model remains comparatively higher in contrast
to the ones identified by the two referred baseline models. Figure 3.6(b), on
the contrary, highlights the number of misbehaving vehicles injected in an IoV
network vis-á-vis the average number of misbehaving vehicles identified by our
envisaged IoV-based trust model and the referred baseline models. It is quite
apparent that regardless of the proportion of the misbehaving vehicles injected

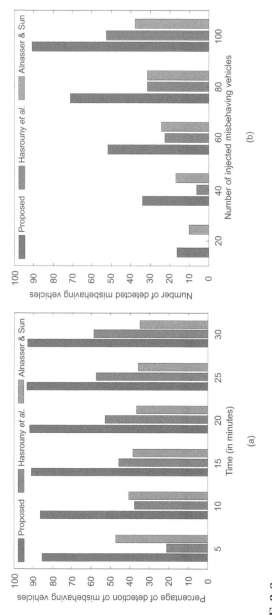

FIGURE 3.6

(a) Average percentage of detection of misbehaving vehicles via our envisaged IoV-based trust model vis-à-vis the baseline models over the simulated time duration, (b) average number of detected misbehaving vehicles vis-à-vis the number of injected misbehaving vehicles in an IoV network via our envisaged IoV-based trust model and the baseline models (baseline models: Hasrouny et al. [28] and Alnasser & Sun [29]).

TABLE 3.3

Average true positive rates pertinent to the misbehaving vehicles' identification ascertained for our envisaged IoV-based trust model, the referred baseline models, i.e., Hasrouny et al. [28] and Alnasser & Sun [29], and Huang et al. [30] vis-á-vis an increase in the arrival rate of the misbehaving vehicles in an IoV network subsequent to an observing time duration of 30 minutes (The average true negative rates pertinent to the honest vehicles' identification for our envisaged IoV-based trust model are $\lambda = 1 : 0.86667$, $\lambda = 2 : 0.83333$, and $\lambda = 3 : 0.76667$. It is pertinent to note that the IoV-based trust models prevalent in the research literature have been traditionally designed by the research community for eliminating the malicious vehicles and, therefore, the significance of the retention of the honest vehicles has been largely ignored in the same, i.e., particularly in Hasrouny et al. [28] and Huang et al. [30]. Needless to mention, the overall cost of entertaining a malicious vehicle in an IoV network is much higher than having an honest vehicle mistakenly removed from the same).

Scheme	$\lambda = 1$	$\lambda = 2$	$\lambda = 3$
Proposed	0.92890	0.87318	0.79366
Hasrouny et al. [28]	0.58560	0.57932	0.54785
Alnasser & Sun [29]	0.34780	0.26815	0.20819
Huang et al. [30]	0.36784	0.34532	0.33729

within an IoV network, the number of misbehaving vehicles detected via our envisaged IoV-based trust model remained consistently higher in contrast to the baseline models.

It is pertinent to highlight that the higher detection rate of our envisaged IoV-based trust model is primarily owing to its timely identification and subsequent elimination of misbehaving vehicles in an IoV network. This, therefore, ensures that the malicious vehicles do not accumulate for too long in an IoV network at any given instance of time. Moreover, it is interesting to note the sheer contrast in the detection rates of both the baseline models, i.e., the detection rate of [28] increases over the simulated time duration and with an increase in the number of injected misbehaving vehicles, and that too, albeit fairly slow owing to (a) its incomprehensive trust evaluation of vehicles in an IoV network and (b) the significantly lower inspection threshold which allows the misbehaving vehicles to remain in the network for a considerable amount of time, and which itself, is extremely contagious for the network. On the contrary, the detection rate of [29] decreases both over the simulated time duration and with an increase in the number of misbehaving vehicles exposing its vulnerable nature.

Table 3.3 further demonstrates the average true positive rates pertinent to the misbehaving vehicles' identification ascertained for our envisaged IoV-based trust model, the referred baseline models, and [30] vis-á-vis an increase in the arrival rate of the misbehaving vehicles within an IoV network subsequent to an observing time duration of 30 minutes. Here, the true positive rate implies the proportion of the misbehaving vehicles correctly identified by the said models. Let λ represents the arrival rate of the misbehaving vehicles in an IoV network, and $\lambda = 1, 2$, and 3 signifies the arrival of one, two, and three misbehaving vehicles, respectively at each time instance. Here, each time instance is manifested in terms of 10 seconds. It can be observed that the true positive rate of our envisaged IoV-based trust model, the referred baseline models, and [30] decrease with an increase in the arrival rate of the misbehaving vehicles. Nevertheless, our envisaged IoV-based trust model still exhibits a higher detection rate in contrast to the said models.

Also, in order to evaluate the resilience of our envisaged IoV-based trust model, we have hereby introduced two different attacks on an IoV network, i.e., a bad-mouthing attack and a self-promoting attack. As discussed earlier, a bad-mouthing attack, also generally referred to as the slandering attack, is one of the most common forms of attacks on the reputation-based networks, wherein malicious vehicles defame the good vehicles by randomly assigning a false (bad) reputation on them in a bid to destroy their reputation subsequently forcing them to be eliminated from the network [43, 48]. On the contrary, in a self-promoting attack, the malicious vehicles falsely enhance their personal reputation by either fabricating a positive feedback about themselves or via altering their feedback during the dissemination. Self-promoting attack may transpire alone or occur as part of an organized group. Networks lacking data authentication and data integrity are more susceptible to such sort of attacks as they are unable to distinguish between the legitimate and the fabricated feedbacks.

Figures 3.7(a) and 3.7(b) accordingly portray the resilience of our envisaged IoV-based trust model against the said attacks. It can be observed that our envisaged IoV-based trust model outperforms both the baseline models in terms of the average percentage of detection of bad-mouthing and self-promoting vehicles over the simulated time duration. This undoubtedly again attests to the considerable significance of the quality attributes of familiarity, content similarity, and timeliness that results in an intelligent weights' assignment for the direct and indirect trust in our envisaged IoV-based trust model. In case of a bad-mouthing attack, while the malicious vehicles launch a collusion-based strategy in a bid to impose a bad reputation on the honest vehicles, the honest vehicles take into consideration the higher reputation segments instead of being misled by the defective reputations segments to flag a malicious behavior. A higher reputation segment is where a trustor has more prior knowledge pertinent to a trustee so that it can make accurate decisions on the opinions disseminated by the trustee. Accordingly, if a malicious vehicle which has just landed in an IoV network or has not operated in the same for too long begins to impose bad reputation on an honest vehicle, then the reputation segments disseminated by such a malicious vehicle, i.e., in the form of indirect trust, would not have any noticeable impact since they would

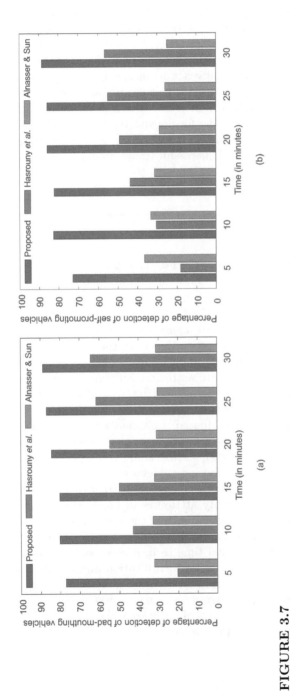

FIGURE 3.7

(a) Average percentage of detection of the bad-mouthing vehicles via our envisaged IoV-based trust model vis-á-vis the baseline models over the simulated time duration, (b) average percentage of detection of the self-promoting vehicles via our envisaged IoV-based trust model vis-á-vis the baseline models over the simulated time duration (baseline models: Hasrouny et al. [28] and Alnasser & Sun [29]).

deem to be of lower quality. In fact, such malicious vehicles would end up getting flagged in the IoV network via a consensus of the honest vehicles. On the other hand, if an intelligent malicious vehicle that has been prevalent in the IoV network has decided to come out of its disguise by becoming part of such a collusion-based attacking strategy, it would also get flagged in no time. It is noteworthy to mention that intelligent malicious vehicles prior to coming out of their disguise usually act haphazardly, i.e., in a cooperative and a non-cooperative manner owing to their nature, and have a credible low opinion pertinent to them already in place. The self-promoting attacks, on the contrary, are handled by looking for unexpected large number of positive feedbacks of a trustee in an IoV network and via requesting accountability on the same in terms of the proof of successful transactions.

3.6 Summary

With the advent of the modern smart cities, the role of intelligent transportation systems is becoming more and more integral for guaranteeing secure and intelligent traffic flows since they facilitate vehicles to interact with several road entities, including but not limited to, other vehicles in their immediate ambience and vulnerable pedestrians, along with the supporting roadside infrastructure via V2X communication so that both the safety-critical and the non-safety vehicular (infotainment) applications could be realized. However, entities in such an IoV network are extremely vulnerable and are susceptible to a diverse range of both external and internal attacks with the later one unable to be determined by the traditional cryptographic-based security techniques. In this chapter, a distributed trust management system has been proposed that takes in account the reputation segments ascertained as a result of a trustor's direct interaction with a trustee and through recommendations obtained from the one-hop neighboring vehicles of the said trustee so as to accurately ascertain its trust score. The envisaged trust management system takes into consideration the quality attributes of familiarity, similarity, and timeliness to determine the weight for each of the reputation segment. An intelligent trust threshold mechanism (with introduction of an inspection threshold and an allocation of additional time to inspected vehicles under specific conditions) has also been proposed for identification and eviction of misbehaving vehicles in an IoV network in an accurate manner. Our experimental results suggest that the proposed trust management system outperforms other state-of-the-art trust models in terms of optimizing the misbehaving vehicles' identification and its resilience to attacks.

Bibliography

[1] Parag Sewalkar and Jochen Seitz. Vehicle-to-Pedestrian Communication for Vulnerable Road Users: Survey, Design Considerations, and Challenges. *Sensors*, 19(2):358, 2019.

[2] Farhan Ahmad, Fatih Kurugollu, Asma Adnane, Rasheed Hussain, and Fatima Hussain. MARINE: Man-in-the-Middle Attack Resistant Trust Model in Connected Vehicles. *IEEE Internet of Things Journal*, 7(4):3310–3322, 2020.

[3] Baofeng Ji, Xueru Zhang, Shahid Mumtaz, Congzheng Han, Chunguo Li, Hong Wen, and Dan Wang. A Survey on the Internet of Vehicles: Network Architectures and Applications. *IEEE Communications Standards Magazine*, 4(1):34–41, 2020.

[4] Longhua Guo, Mianxiong Dong, Kaoru Ota, Qiang Li, Tianpeng Ye, Jun Wu, and Jianhua Li. A Secure Mechanism for Big Data Collection in Large Scale Internet of Vehicle. *IEEE Internet of Things Journal*, 4(2):601–610, 2017.

[5] Xiaoya Xu, Yunpeng Wang, Pengcheng Wang, and Haojie Ji. A Secure and Efficient Authentication Scheme in the Internet of Vehicle Communication. *Personal and Ubiquitous Computing*, 2021.

[6] Amal Hbaieb, Samiha Ayed, and L. Chaari. A Survey of Trust Management in the Internet of Vehicles. *Computer Networks*, 203:108558, 2022.

[7] Adnan Mahmood, Wei Emma Zhang, and Quan Z. Sheng. Software-Defined Heterogeneous Vehicular Networking: The Architectural Design and Open Challenges. *Future Internet*, 11(3):70, 2019.

[8] Hamideh Fatemidokht, Marjan Kuchaki Rafsanjani, Brij B. Gupta, and Ching-Hsien Hsu. Efficient and Secure Routing Protocol based on Artificial Intelligence Algorithms with UAV-Assisted for Vehicular Ad Hoc Networks in Intelligent Transportation Systems. *IEEE Transactions on Intelligent Transportation Systems*, 22(7):1–13, 2021.

[9] Haibin Zhang, Jiajia Liu, Huanlei Zhao, Peng Wang, and Nei Kato. Blockchain-based Trust Management for Internet of Vehicles. *IEEE Transactions on Emerging Topics in Computing*, 9(3):1397–1409, 2021.

[10] Sameer Qazi, Farah Sabir, Bilal A. Khawaja, Syed Muhammad Atif, and Muhammad Mustaqim. Why Is Internet of Autonomous Vehicles Not As Plug and Play As We Think ? Lessons to Be Learnt From Present Internet and Future Directions. *IEEE Access*, 8:133015–133033, 2020.

[11] Dajiang Suo and Sanjay E. Sarma. Real-time Trust-Building Schemes for Mitigating Malicious Behaviors in Connected & Automated Vehicles. In *2019 IEEE Intelligent Transportation Systems Conference (ITSC)*, pages 1142–1149, Auckland, New Zealand, 2019. IEEE.

[12] Hesham El Sayed, Sherali Zeadally, and Deepak Puthal. Design and Evaluation of a Novel Hierarchical Trust Assessment Approach for Vehicular Networks. *Vehicular Communications*, 24:100227, 2020.

[13] Aljawharah Alnasser, Hongjian Sun, and Jing Jiang. Recommendation-based Trust Model for Vehicle-to-Everything (V2X). *IEEE Internet of Things Journal*, 7(1):440–450, 2020.

[14] Adnan Mahmood, Quan Z. Sheng, Wei Emma Zhang, Yan Wang, and Subhash Sagar. Towards a Distributed Trust Management System for Misbehavior Detection in the Internet of Vehicles. *ACM Trans. Cyber-Phys. Syst.*, 2023. Just Accepted.

[15] Rasheed Hussain, Jooyoung Lee, and Sherali Zeadally. Trust in VANET: A Survey of Current Solutions and Future Research Opportunities. *IEEE Transactions on Intelligent Transportation Systems*, 22(5):2553–2571, 2021.

[16] Gagan Preet Kour Marwah and Anuj Jain. A Hybrid Optimization with Ensemble Learning to Ensure VANET Network Stability based on Performance Analysis. *Scientific Reports (Nature Portfolio)*, 12(1):10287, 2022.

[17] Sofia Azam, Maryum Bibi, Rabia Riaz, Sanam Shahla Rizvi, and Se Jin Kwon. Collaborative Learning Based Sybil Attack Detection in Vehicular AD-HOC Networks (VANETS). *Sensors*, 22(18):6934, Sep 2022.

[18] Jin-Hee Cho, Ananthram Swami, and Ing-Ray Chen. A Survey on Trust Management for Mobile Ad Hoc Networks. *IEEE Communications Surveys & Tutorials*, 13(4):562–583, 2011.

[19] Ing-Ray Chen and Jia Guo. Dynamic Hierarchical Trust Management of Mobile Groups and Its Application to Misbehaving Node Detection. In *2014 IEEE 28th International Conference on Advanced Information Networking and Applications*, pages 49–56, Victoria, BC, Canada, 2014. IEEE.

[20] Hui Xia, Zhetao Li, Yuhui Zheng, Anfeng Liu, Young-June Choi, and Hiroo Sekiya. A Novel Light-Weight Subjective Trust Inference Framework in MANETs. *IEEE Transactions on Sustainable Computing*, 5(2):236–248, 2020.

[21] Michail Chatzidakis and Stathes Hadjiefthymiades. A Trust Change Detection Mechanism in Mobile Ad-hoc Networks. *Computer Communications*, 187:155–163, 2022.

[22] Farhan Ahmad, Virginia N. L. Franqueira, and Asma Adnane. TEAM: A Trust Evaluation and Management Framework in Context-Enabled Vehicular Ad-Hoc Networks. *IEEE Access*, 6:28643–28660, 2018.

[23] Sohan Gyawali, Yi Qian, and Rose Qingyang Hu. Machine Learning and Reputation Based Misbehavior Detection in the Vehicular Communication Networks. *IEEE Transactions on Vehicular Technology*, 69(8):8871–8885, 2020.

[24] Sabine Frittella, Krishna Manoorkar, Alessandra Palmigiano, Apostolos Tzimoulis, and Nachoem Wijnberg. Toward a Dempster-Shafer Theory of Concepts. *International Journal of Approximate Reasoning*, 125:14–25, 2020.

[25] Jiliang Li, Rui Xing, Zhou Su, Ning Zhang, Yilong Hui, Tom H. Luan, and Hangguan Shan. Trust Based Secure Content Delivery in Vehicular Networks: A Bargaining Game Theoretical Approach. *IEEE Transactions on Vehicular Technology*, 69(3):3267–3279, 2020.

[26] Chaker Abdelaziz Kerrache, Nasreddine Lagraa, Rasheed Hussain, Syed Hassan Ahmed, Abderrahim Benslimane, Carlos T. Calafate, Juan-Carlos Cano, and Anna Maria Vegni. TACASHI: Trust-Aware Communication Architecture for Social Internet of Vehicles. *IEEE Internet of Things Journal*, 6(4):5870–5877, 2019.

[27] Siri Guleng, Celimuge Wu, Xianfu Chen, Xiaoyan Wang, Tsutomu Yoshinaga, and Yusheng Ji. Decentralized Trust Evaluation in Vehicular Internet of Things. *IEEE Access*, 7:15980–15988, 2019.

[28] Hamssa Hasrouny, Abed Ellatif Samhat, Carole Bassil, and Anis Laouiti. Trust Model for Secure Group Leader-based Communications in VANET. *Wireless Networks*, 25(8):4639–4661, 2019.

[29] Aljawharah Alnasser and Hongjian Sun. Global Roaming Trust-based Model for V2X Communications. In *IEEE INFOCOM WKSHPS 2019 - IEEE Conference on Computer Communications Workshops (INFOCOM WKSHPS)*, pages 1–6, Paris, France, 2019. IEEE.

[30] Xumin Huang, Rong Yu, Jiawen Kang, and Yan Zhang. Distributed Reputation Management for Secure and Efficient Vehicular Edge Computing and Networks. *IEEE Access*, 5:25408–25420, 2017.

[31] Claudia-Lavinia Ignat, Quang-Vinh Dang, and Valerie L. Shalin. The Influence of Trust Score on Cooperative Behavior. *ACM Trans. Internet Technology*, 19(4), September 2019.

[32] Pasquale De Meo. Trust Prediction via Matrix Factorisation. *ACM Trans. Internet Technol.*, 19(4), September 2019.

[33] Zhengdi Hu, Guangquan Xu, Xi Zheng, Jiang Liu, Zhangbing Li, Quan Z. Sheng, Wenjuan Lian, and Hequn Xian. SSL-SVD: Semi-Supervised Learning–Based Sparse Trust Recommendation. *ACM Trans. Internet Technol.*, 20(1), January 2020.

[34] George Hatzivasilis, Othonas Soultatos, Sotiris Ioannidis, George Spanoudakis, Vasilios Katos, and Giorgos Demetriou. MobileTrust: Secure Knowledge Integration in VANETs. *ACM Transactions on Cyber-Physical Systems*, 4(3), March 2020.

[35] Adnan Mahmood, Sarah Ali Siddiqui, Quan Z. Sheng, Wei Emma Zhang, Hajime Suzuki, and Wei Ni. Trust on Wheels: Towards Secure and Resource Efficient IoV Networks. *Computing*, 104(6):1337–1358, 2022.

[36] Adnan Mahmood, Quan Z. Sheng, Sarah Ali Siddiqui, Subhash Sagar, Wei Emma Zhang, Hajime Suzuki, and Wei Ni. When Trust Meets the Internet of Vehicles: Opportunities, Challenges, and Future Prospects. In *2021 IEEE 7th International Conference on Collaboration and Internet Computing (CIC)*, pages 60–67, Atlanta, GA, USA, 2021. IEEE.

[37] Sarah Ali Siddiqui, Adnan Mahmood, Quan Z. Sheng, Hajime Suzuki, and Wei Ni. A Survey of Trust Management in the Internet of Vehicles. *Electronics*, 10(18):2223, 2021.

[38] Razi Iqbal, Talal Ashraf Butt, Muhammad Afzaal, and Khaled Salah. Trust Management in Social Internet of Vehicles: Factors, Challenges, Blockchain, and Fog Solutions. *International Journal of Distributed Sensor Networks*, 15(1), 2019.

[39] Shibin Wang and Nianmin Yao. A RSU-aided Distributed Trust Framework for Pseudonym-enabled Privacy Preservation in VANETs. *Wireless Networks*, 25(3):1099–1115, 2019.

[40] Jin Wang, Yonghui Zhang, Youyuan Wang, and Xiang Gu. RPRep: A Robust and Privacy-Preserving Reputation Management Scheme for Pseudonym-Enabled VANETs. *International Journal of Distributed Sensor Networks*, 12(3), 2016.

[41] Mohammad Khayatian, Mohammadreza Mehrabian, Edward Andert, Rachel Dedinsky, Sarthake Choudhary, Yingyan Lou, and Aviral Shirvastava. A Survey on Intersection Management of Connected Autonomous Vehicles. *ACM Transactions on Cyber-Physical Systems*, 4(4), August 2020.

[42] Fangyu Gai, Jiexin Zhang, Peidong Zhu, and Xinwen Jiang. Trust on the Ratee: A Trust Management System for Social Internet of Vehicles. *Wireless Communications and Mobile Computing*, 2017, 2017.

[43] Jinsong Zhang, Kangfeng Zheng, Dongmei Zhang, and Bo Yan. AATMS: An Anti-Attack Trust Management Scheme in VANET. *IEEE Access*, 8:21077–21090, 2020.

[44] Farhan Ahmad, Asma Adnane, Chaker A. Kerrache, Fatih Kurugollu, and Iain Phillips. On the Design, Development, and Implementation of Trust Evaluation Mechanism in Vehicular Networks. In *2019 IEEE/ACS 16th International Conference on Computer Systems and Applications (AICCSA)*, pages 1–7, Abu Dhabi, United Arab Emirates, 2019. IEEE.

[45] Farhan Ahmad, Fatih Kurugollu, Chaker Abdelaziz Kerrache, Sakir Sezer, Lu Liu. NOTRINO: a NOvel hybrid TRust management scheme for INternet-Of-vehicles. *IEEE Transactions on Vehicular Technology*, 70(9), 2021.

[46] Ji-Ming Chen, Ting-Ting Li, John Panneerselvam. TMEC: A Trust Management Based on Evidence Combination on Attack-Resistant and Collaborative Internet of Vehicles. *IEEE Access*, 7:148913–148922, 2019.

[47] Carolina V. L. Mendoza and João H. Kleinschmidt. Defense for Selective Attacks in the IoT with a Distributed Trust Management Scheme. In *2016 IEEE International Symposium on Consumer Electronics (ISCE)*, pages 53–54, Sao Paulo, Brazil, 2016. IEEE.

[48] Kevin Hoffman, David Zage, and Cristina Nita-Rotaru. A Survey of Attack and Defense Techniques for Reputation Systems. *ACM Computing Surveys*, 42(1), December 2009.

[49] William Stallings. *Computer Organization and Architecture – Designing for Performance*. Pearson Education, Inc., Hoboken, NJ, 11th edition, 2019.

[50] Yining Liu, Keqiu Li, Yong Zhang, and Wenyu Qu. A Novel Reputation Computation Model Based on Subjective Logic for Mobile Ad Hoc Networks. In *2009 Third International Conference on Network and System Security*, pages 294–301, Gold Coast, QLD, Australia, 2009. IEEE.

[51] Audun Jøsang. A Logic for Uncertain Probabilities. *International Journal of Uncertainty, Fuzziness and Knowledge-Based Systems*, 9(3):279–311, 2001.

[52] Besat Jafarian, Nasser Yazdani, and Mohammad Sayad Haghighi. Discrimination-aware Trust Management for Social Internet of Things. *Computer Networks*, 178, 2020.

[53] Iván García-Magariño, Sandra Sendra, Raquel Lacuesta, and Jaime Lloret. Security in Vehicles with IoT by Prioritization Rules, Vehicle Certificates, and Trust Management. *IEEE Internet of Things Journal*, 6(4):5927–5934, 2019.

[54] Honghao Gao, Can Liu, Yuyu Yin, Yueshen Xu, and Yu Li. A Hybrid Approach to the Trust Node Assessment and Management for VANETs Cooperative Data Communication: Historical Interaction Perspective. *IEEE Transactions on Intelligent Transportation Systems*, 23(9):16504–16513, 2022.

4

Towards Secure and Resource Efficient IoV Networks: A Hybrid Trust Management Approach

The emerging yet promising paradigm of Internet-of-Vehicles (IoV) has received considerable attention in the recent years as an integral and indispensable constituent of the modern intelligent transportation systems, wherein safety-critical information is exchanged amongst the connected vehicles via a high-bandwidth, low-latent vehicle-to-everything communication system so as to ensure road safety and highly efficient traffic flows. Therefore, it is of utmost importance to ensure the authenticity and reliability of such safety messages together with the legitimacy of the vehicles disseminating the same. This necessitates instituting a state-of-the-art trust-based mechanism in order to not only identify but to further evict the malicious vehicles from an IoV network. The risk augments if a malicious vehicle (via its malign attempts) assume the role of a cluster head in a cluster, thereby jeopardizing the safety of both the occupants of the vehicles and vulnerable pedestrians. Hence, intelligent algorithms with a potential to opt for both a trusted and a resource efficient cluster head needs to be put into place to guarantee the overall security and resource efficacy of the corresponding cluster. Accordingly, in this chapter, we have envisaged a scalable hybrid trust-based model which introduces a composite metric encompassing the weighted amalgamation of a vehicle's computed trust score and its corresponding available resources in order to ensure that the stringent performance requirements of the safety-critical vehicular applications are fully met. A Hungarian algorithm-based role assignment mechanism has been subsequently envisaged for the selection of an optimal cluster head, proxy cluster head, and followers amongst the members of a vehicular cluster for maximizing its overall efficacy. Furthermore, the notion of an adaptive threshold has been proposed in order to identify and subsequently eliminate the smart malicious vehicles from an IoV network in a timely manner, i.e., as soon as they start exhibiting an adverse behavior, to guarantee that the network is not manipulated for any malicious gains. Extensive simulations have been carried out and performance analysis demonstrates the efficaciousness of our proposed scheme.

DOI: 10.1201/9781003365037-4

4.1 Introduction

Over the past few decades or so, the promising notion of Internet-of-Vehicles (IoV) has been extensively studied by researchers in both academia and industry. As-of-today, vehicles employ vehicle-to-vehicle communication in a bid to exchange safety and non-safety, i.e., infotainment, messages with one another, vehicle-to-infrastructure and vehicle-to-network communication to communicate with the supporting roadside infrastructure, i.e., traffic lights and parking spaces, and with the backbone network (data centers), respectively, and vehicle-to-pedestrian communication to interact with the smartphone-toting vulnerable pedestrians. All of this falls under the umbrella of Vehicle-to-Everything (V2X) communication, wherein information propagates via a high-bandwidth, low-latent link to ensure highly secure and intelligent traffic flows [1, 2, 3]. All of this is also integral to the futuristic 5G networks and is highly indispensable for the technological evolution of connected and autonomous vehicles and smart cities. Nevertheless, safety-critical communication in an IoV context could not be realized until the network is completely secure since the dissemination of even a *'single'* malicious message may not only jeopardizes the entire network but could further transpire in a number of fatalities on the road [4]. It is, therefore, of the utmost importance that the malicious entities (and their messages) be identified and subsequently eliminated from a network before they are able to manipulate the entire network for their own malicious gains [5, 6, 7].

Accordingly, numerous research studies have been proposed over the years for ensuring security in a vehicular networking context [8, 9, 10, 11, 12, 13]. Existing schemes primarily tend to focus on the conventional cryptographic-based solutions utilizing certificates and public key infrastructure as to guarantee security for vehicular networks. Nevertheless, cryptographic-based schemes are not optimal for an IoV network considering the highly dynamic and distributed nature of an IoV network, the lack of a pervasive networking infrastructure, and the vulnerability of cryptography-based techniques to insider attacks [14, 15, 16]. Hence, in order to ensure the security within an IoV network, the notion of *trust* has been off lately introduced by researchers from both academia and industry and which itself manifests *'the confidence of one vehicle on the other'.*

Trust establishment among vehicles facilitate in revoking of dishonest vehicles by assessing the authenticity and correctness of the information originated via them. Furthermore, it is pertinent to highlight that the existing trust-based schemes are based on a stable adversary behavior, wherein it is assumed that a malicious vehicle always act in a dishonest manner. In fact, a malicious vehicle could act *smartly* and disguise between an honest and a dishonest behavior so as to avoid detection from the neighboring vehicles and both the localized and centralized network traffic monitoring authorities. It is, therefore, of extreme importance to identify smart malicious vehicles before they begin operating in the disguise mode in order to mitigate their potential threats to a network. Moreover, vehicles may also manifest a *selfish* behavior, wherein they only act (i.e., participate in the network) when it best serves their own interest [17, 18].

It is also noteworthy to mention that connected vehicles in an IoV network organize themselves in the form of vehicular groups, i.e., clusters, when traversing on the road. The group leaders, also referred to as the cluster heads, are in charge of communicating between the clusters (inter-cluster communication), amongst the vehicles of their respective cluster (intra-cluster communication), along with reporting an entire cluster's status to the backbone network in a bid to alleviate the network management overhead. Hence, considering the significance of a cluster head's role in a cluster, opting a suitable vehicle for the role of a cluster head is highly indispensable as a dishonest vehicle governing the entire cluster would yield grave consequences for the network and its users. Nevertheless, possessing a highest trust score does not necessarily justifies a vehicle's eligibility as a cluster head. In fact, apart from being categorized as a trustworthy one, a vehicle that can guarantee the efficacy of the entire cluster is considered as an optimal choice for the role of a cluster head. To the best of our knowledge, the existing literature has not catered for the same in its true essence. Accordingly, our contributions in this chapter are threefold [19]:

- A scalable hybrid trust model has been envisaged that introduces a composite metric encompassing the weighted amalgamation of a vehicle's computed trust score and its corresponding available resources to guarantee that the stringent performance requirements for the safety-critical vehicular applications are fully met,

- A Hungarian algorithm-based optimal role assignment scheme has been envisaged for the selection of an optimal cluster head, proxy cluster head, and followers amongst the members of a vehicular cluster in order to maximize its overall efficacy, and

- The notion of an adaptive threshold has been proposed in order to identify and subsequently eliminate smart malicious vehicles from an IoV network in a timely manner, i.e., as soon as they begin to demonstrate an adverse sort of a behavior, so as to ensure that the IoV network is not manipulated for any malicious gains.

The rest of this chapter is organized as follows. Section 4.2 outlines the state-of-the-art pertinent to trust-based frameworks within an IoV context. Section 4.3 delineates on the envisaged hybrid trust model, cluster head selection mechanism, and an adaptive threshold scheme. Section 4.4 describes the simulation results and features performance analysis, whereas, the last section, i.e., Section 4.5, concludes the research-at-hand and discusses future research directions.

4.2   The State of the Art

Although a considerable amount of research efforts have already been invested into IoV networks by researchers from both academia and industry, it has not yet been fully commercialized partially owing to the challenges pertinent to its security and privacy. As of date, a number of IoV-related security aspects have been extensively deliberated in the research literature, including but not limited to, authentication, integrity, confidentiality, non-repudiation, availability, scalability, misbehavior detection (and mitigation), and forward and backward secrecy [4, 20]. Existing security solutions are generally classified into two broad categories, i.e., cryptography and trust. Although the cryptographic-based solutions are considered as the first line of defense against a number of network attacks, they alone cannot address all the security aspects of an IoV network, and therefore, trust management is employed as an additional level of security in a bid to overcome the shortcomings of the conventional cryptographic-based solutions, i.e., in particular against the inside attackers in possession of valid certificates [21]. Furthermore, several research studies integrating blockchain with IoV have been recently proposed in the literature primarily as blockchain possesses the capability of guaranteeing data immutability [22]. Nevertheless, a number of inherent challenges still need to be intelligently addressed in this regard. For instance, the number of transactions required to update the ledger between the vehicles and the blockchain network are extremely high and could end up consuming the maximum available energy [23, 24]. Similarly, blockchain mechanisms utilize public key operations which may result in excessive overhead in the case of blockchain-enabled IoV networks, i.e., even if lightweight cryptographic algorithms have been employed for onboard security. Since this chapter delineates on the notion of trust management within the context of IoV networks, we would subsequently elaborate on its state-of-the-art.

A brief overview of the existing literature depicts a wide variety of research studies suggesting the trust management frameworks in a vehicular networking environment. In [8], a stable and an efficacious trust-based clustering scheme has been envisaged for an IoV network, wherein the roadside units via a centralized approach ascertains and maintains the trust value for all the vehicles in their respective coverage area. Once a vehicle has been categorized as either malicious or compromised, the respective RSU blocks it by communicating its particulars with the other vehicles and further stops it from becoming part of any neighboring cluster. The trust of any vehicle and the selection of a cluster head is primarily dependent on the trust attributes of knowledge, reputation, and experience and a vehicle possessing superior trust, i.e., above a trust score of *0.8* (on a trust scale of *0–1*), gets the priority to become the cluster head. A backup cluster head is also selected for stabilizing the cluster, i.e., if the cluster head is compromised, does not perform its due responsibilities, or surrenders, then the backup cluster head takes up the role of a cluster head.

In [9] and [10], the authors proposed a trust-based clustering mechanism for a vehicular networking environment. The said mechanism encompasses two key stages, (a) a cluster formation process, wherein a cluster is formed of vehicles traversing with similar velocity features and a common vehicle in the restricted neighborhood of all vehicles is subsequently elected as the cluster head and (b) a cluster maintenance step, wherein a cluster is maintained primarily owing to the rapid changes in the network topology transpiring as a consequence of the arrival, displacement, or even failure of a vehicle. The cluster head is primarily responsible for ascertaining the reputation for each vehicle depending on the quality and accuracy of the messages it reports to a cluster head intimating it of an event. Overtime, the cluster head employs this reputation for determining if a subsequent message reported to it by the corresponding vehicle should be dropped or broadcast to the RSUs, member of a cluster, or to other clusters.

In [11], a clustering protocol has been proposed for electing both stable and trustworthy cluster heads in the vehicular ad hoc networks (VANETs) primarily via employing a hybrid mechanism encompassing stability, i.e., ascertained in terms of the degree of similarity of mobility metrics, and trust factors, i.e., depending on both the data trust and the communication trust. During the initialization phase, each vehicle broadcasts a 'hello message' within the network comprising its ID, speed, acceleration, and position in order to formulate (or update) its neighboring table. Once all of the vehicles have formulated (or updated) their neighboring tables, they ascertain their respective scores in terms of their relative speed, distance, and acceleration vis-á-vis their corresponding neighbors. Therefore, a vehicle with nearly identical speed and acceleration to that of its neighbors and possessing the maximum number of neighbors should possess a maximum score. Furthermore, an intelligent backoff time mechanism has been envisaged by the authors so as to minimize the control traffic during the clustering process by primarily eliminating the competition of vehicles to become a clusterhead. Each vehicle subsequently launches a timer which is inversely proportional to its score implying that a vehicle with the highest score would have the smallest timer and, therefore, it declares itself as a candidate for the cluster head.

A dedicated trust-based security scheme for exchanging messages in VANETs has been envisaged in [12], wherein the authors conceived a vehicular grouping algorithm comprising three key phases, i.e., pre-processing, setup, and maintenance. The initial reputations are hence allocated to the vehicles depending on the exchanged credentials amongst them and which are themselves segregated into three groups, i.e., most sensitive, normally sensitive, and less sensitive. A node that is able to share more sensitive particulars is hence assigned a higher trust score. In the setup phase, groups, i.e., clusters, are formed and a group head is subsequently elected primarily owing to its highest reputation score. Finally, the maintenance phase responds to all topological changes transpiring due to leaving of a group member or group head or arrival of a new vehicle in a network. A trust management scheme, built on the top of grouping algorithm, has been further proposed for handling the messages exchanged in a vehicular networking environment. The veracity of any alert message is ascertained via three indicators, i.e., the location closeness, time closeness depicting the freshness of a message, and sender's reputation. An inference system has also been designed for validating the soundness and the completeness of the envisaged trust-based security scheme.

In [13], a trust-based authentication scheme has been proposed for cluster-based VANETs, wherein vehicles are organized in the form of clusters and the trust of each vehicle is ascertained in light of the direct trust and indirect trust. The cluster heads are subsequently selected depending on the estimated trust degree which is a weighted sum of both direct trust and indirect trust. Moreover, a set of verifier vehicles observe the behavior of each vehicle in a cluster and the ones possessing a malicious behavior are isolated by a certification authority. The digitally signed messages by the sender are further encrypted via a public/private key and then decrypted at the destination, thereby verifying the identity of both the sender and the receiver.

Nevertheless, all of these above-referred schemes have some inherent shortcomings, i.e., either they rely on a centralized authority to ascertain and maintain the trust of all vehicles in a network and which itself results in an excessive network management overhead primarily in the case of a dense road network scenario or assigns the role of a cluster head to a vehicle possessing the highest trust score. Similarly, some of these referred schemes select a cluster head primarily on the premise of similar mobility features and the cluster head subsequently ascertains the reputation of its members in order to determine their fate. This can prove risky in case a vehicle with an adverse or a selfish behavior end up becoming a cluster head as it could manipulate the entire network for its own malicious gains, and in worst scenarios, could prove fatal for both the occupants of the vehicles and the vulnerable pedestrians.

It is also pertinent to mention that there are a number of attacks that could affect the trustworthiness of vehicles to a considerable extent, thereby impacting their authenticity in an IoV network. Some of such attacks include, but are not limited to, self-promoting attacks, selective behavior attacks, opportunistic service attacks, on-off attacks, ballot stuffing attacks, and the bad mouthing attacks [25, 26]. The self-promoting attacks, selective behavior attacks, opportunistic service attacks, and on-off attacks represent the class of attacks which are primarily based on self-interest. On the contrary, the ballot stuffing attacks and bad mouthing attacks are categorized as reputation-based attacks [27, 28]. This further highlights the need of intelligent misbehavior detection techniques which should be capable of identifying a diverse range of simultaneous attacks and dynamic attackers' strategies under varying contexts.

4.3 The System Model

4.3.1 Trust Scores Assignment

We, hereby, define a set of vehicles V_n, encompassing both honest as well as dishonest vehicles, where $n = \{1,\ldots,N\}$. At every time instance $t, t = \{1,\ldots,T\}$, each vehicle communicates, i.e., interacts, with the other vehicles in its immediate ambience, and accordingly, evaluate one another on the basis of messages exchanged between them. The said evaluations transpire in the form of a pair/set of a trustor j and a trustee i (wherein, $j \neq i$), i.e., between a vehicle carrying out the trust evaluation and the one being evaluated, respectively. As a consequence of the said evaluations, trust values $T_{seg_{i,j,t}}$ are assigned to each trustee i by all of its neighboring, i.e., $N-1$, trustors within its immediate ambience with whom it interacts while it traverses within the network. Each trustee, therefore, ends up having $N-1$ distinct trust scores $T_{seg_{i,j,t}}$ assigned to it, generally referred to as reputation segments, which are subsequently averaged out in order to acquire a single trust score $T_{avg_{i,t}}$ for each trustee in a vehicular network.

Each reputation segment $T_{seg_{i,j,t}}$ is an amalgamation of (a) the direct trust $\sum_{t'=1}^{t} w_{t'} T_{D_{i,j,t'}}$ ascertained by the weighted sum of all the interactions among a trustor and a trustee, and (b) the indirect trust $\sum_{j'=1}^{N-2} w_{j'} T_{N_{i,j',t}}$ ascertained via the weighted sum of all the one-hop neighbors' recommendations (opinions) pertinent to a trustee. Both $T_{D_{i,j,t'}}$ and $T_{N_{i,j',t}}$ are assigned to a trustee keeping into consideration its conduct in a vehicular network and varies between 0 and 1. Here, 0 manifests an untrusted vehicle at any time instance and 1 represents the trustworthy vehicle.

The trust value assigned to each vehicle by its one-hop neighbors at a single time instance is derived using Equation 4.1 as follows:

$$T_{seg_{i,j,t}} = w_D \sum_{t'=1}^{t} w_{t'} T_{D_{i,j,t'}} + w_N \sum_{j'=1}^{N-2} w_{j'} T_{N_{i,j',t}} \qquad (4.1)$$

where, t' ranges from $1 \leq t' \leq t$ and signifies the interactions of any one-hop neighboring vehicle with a targeted vehicle up to the current time instance t (direct observations), $w_{t'}$ relates to the weightage of the respective t'^{th} interaction (weights $w_{t'}$ sum up to 1), and $T_{D_{i,j,t'}}$ is the trust score ascertained for a targeted vehicle at that respective t'^{th} interaction. This suggests that we are not merely overwriting the earlier direct trust values, i.e., among a trustor and a trustee, rather, the impact of the earlier direct observations is further taken into account, but to some extent, as we are more interested in the recent direct observations in contrast to the earlier direct observations. Hence, a smoothing update procedure [29] has been undertaken for this purpose. Furthermore, N signifies the total number of vehicles in a cluster and

$T_{N_{i,j',t}}$ refers to the trust scores recommended for the targeted vehicle via its $N-2$ one-hop neighboring vehicles, wherein j' is subset of vehicles without a trustor and a trustee (indirect observations), and $w_{j'}$ depicts weightage of a neighbor's recommendation (weights $w_{j'} = 1/|j'|$ sum up to 1). Both weights, w_D and w_N, are ascertained by a local authority which is employed in order to achieve a distributed reputation management. These weights take into consideration the notions of (a) *familiarity* – how well a one-hop neighbor possess a prior knowledge pertinent to a targeted vehicle, (b) *similarity* – the degree of similar content accessed by a trustor and a trustee, and (c) *timeliness* – how recently a neighbor's opinion was formed about a targeted vehicle [30, 31].

The average trust value $T_{avg_{i,t}}$ assigned by the one-hop neighboring vehicles for each of the targeted vehicle at each time instance is ascertained as:

$$T_{avg_{i,t}} = (\sum_{j=1}^{N-1} T_{seg_{i,j,t}})/|N-1| \qquad (4.2)$$

Moreover, a trustworthiness threshold (T_{TH}) has been defined for the identification of the trustworthy vehicles at each time instance t, i.e., if the average trust ($T_{avg_{i,t}}$) of any vehicle i at a time instance is higher than the pre-defined threshold, i.e., $T_{avg_{i,t}} > T_{TH}$, then the vehicle is tagged as a trusted vehicle at that particular time instance as depicted in Equation 4.3:

$$Decision = \begin{cases} Trusted, & \text{if } T_{avg_{i,t}} \geq T_{TH}. \\ Malicious, & \text{otherwise.} \end{cases} \qquad (4.3)$$

4.3.2 Available Resources and Composite Metric Computation

In addition to ascertaining the trust for each vehicle i, the available resources $R_{i,t}$ at a vehicle's disposal are also computed in order to determine if a vehicle i possess considerable resources and thus fulfils the minimum requirement (i.e., $R_{i,t} \geq R_{TH}$, wherein R_{TH} manifests the minimum acceptable threshold) for being a cluster head. The available resources for each vehicle in an IoV network encompasses normalized values of *Available Bandwidth* ($R_{i,t}^{\text{BW}}$) and *Remaining Power* ($R_{i,t}^{\text{P}}$) and is computed via Equation 4.4:

$$R_{i,t} = w_{BW} R_{i,t}^{\text{BW}} + w_P R_{i,t}^{\text{P}}$$

$$w_{BW} + w_P = 1 \qquad (4.4)$$

Lastly, a weighted composition of the computed trust score $T_{avg_{i,t}}$ (as depicted in Section 3.1) and the available resources $R_{i,t}$ is subsequently ascertained for every vehicle i at every time instance t to obtain a composite metric as illustrated in Equation 4.5. The weights, $w_{T_{avg}}$ and w_R, associated

---

Algorithm 1 Composite metric computation

1: **for** $t = 1\,to\,T$ **do**
2:    **for** $i = 1\,to\,N$ **do**
3:       **for** $j = 1\,to\,N$ **do**
4:          **if** $j \neq i$ **then**
5:             **for** $t' = 1\,to\,t$ **do**
6:                $T_{D_{i,j,t'}} \leftarrow Direct\_Interaction\_Trust$
7:                $w_{t'} \leftarrow Interaction\_Weight$
8:                $DT_{i,j,t} \leftarrow Sum(w_{t'}^{*}T_{D_{i,j,t'}})$
9:             **end for**
10:             **for** $j' = 1\,to\,N - 2$ **do**
11:                $T_{N_{i,j',t}} \leftarrow Recommendation\_Trust$
12:                $w_{j'} \leftarrow Recommendation\_Weight$
13:                $IDT_{i,j,t} \leftarrow Sum(w_{j'}^{*}T_{N_{i,j',t}})$
14:             **end for**
15:             $w_D \leftarrow Direct\_Trust\_Weight(f_t, s_t, tl_t)$
16:             $w_N \leftarrow Indirect\_Trust\_Weight(f_t, s_t, tl_t)$
17:             $T_{seg_{i,j,t}} \leftarrow Weighted\_Sum(w_D, DT_{i,j,t}, w_N, IDT_{i,j,t})$
18:          **end if**
19:       **end for**
20:       $T_{avg_{i,t}} \leftarrow Avg(T_{seg_{i,j,t}})$
21:       $R_{i,t} \leftarrow Available\_Resources(w_{BW}, R_{i,t}^{\mathrm{BW}}, w_P, R_{i,t}^{\mathrm{P}})$
22:       $w_R \leftarrow Weight\_Resources$
23:       $w_{T_{avg}} \leftarrow 1 - w_R$
24:       $T_{Metric_{i,t}} \leftarrow Comp\_Metric(w_{T_{avg}}, T_{avg_{i,t}}, w_R, R_{i,t})$
25:    **end for**
26: **end for**

---

with each of these two parameters take into account the vehicular applications' requirements in such a way that $w_{T_{avg}}$ is assigned a higher value in case a vehicular application demands higher security, whereas, for the resource dependant applications, w_R gets assigned a higher value.

$$T_{Metric_{i,t}} = w_{T_{avg}}T_{avg_{i,t}} + w_R R_{i,t}$$

$$w_{T_{avg}} + w_R = 1 \tag{4.5}$$

The proposed composite metric is delineated in detail in Algorithm 1.

4.3.3   Cluster Head Selection

Clustering is a technique for segregating a given network by grouping its participating nodes into diverse groups, wherein a group leader, i.e., often referred as the cluster head, is elected for each group. The cluster head is responsible for ensuring highly trustworthy and efficient inter- and intra-group

---

Algorithm 2 Hungarian-based optimal role assignment scheme

 1: **Input:** Hungarian Cost Matrix $C(i, j)$
 2: **Output:** $Role_1, Role_2, Role_3$
 3: $lines \leftarrow 0$
 4: $p_x \leftarrow 0$
 5: $v \leftarrow number\_of\_vehicles$
 6: $n \leftarrow number\_of\_roles$
 7: $Hungarian(i, j) \leftarrow max(C) - C(i, j)$
 8: **for** $i = 1 \, to \, v$ **do**
 9:     $Hungarian(i, :) \leftarrow Hungarian(i, :) - min(Hungarian(i, :))$
10: **end for**
11: **for** $j = 1 \, to \, n$ **do**
12:     $Hungarian(:, j) \leftarrow Hungarian(:, j) - min(Hungarian(:, j))$
13: **end for**
14: **for** $i = 1 \, to \, v$ **do**
15:     $z \leftarrow size(find(Hungarian(i, :) == 0), 2)$
16:     **if** $z > 0 \ and \ z \leq v$ **then**
17:         **for** $x = 1 \, to \, z$ **do**
18:             $p_x \leftarrow find(Hungarian(i, p_x + 1 : end) == 0, 1)$
19:             $rowp_x \leftarrow i$
20:         **end for**
21:     **end if**
22: **end for**
23: $lines \leftarrow min\_lines$
24: **if** $lines < v$ **then**
25:     **while** $lines < v$ **do**
26:         **for** $i = 1 \, to \, v$ **do**
27:             **for** $j = 1 \, to \, n$ **do**
28:                 $Hungarian(i, j) \leftarrow Hungarian(i, j) - min(Hungarian)$
29:             **end for**
30:         **end for**
31:         Repeat *steps 14 to 23*
32:     **end while**
33: **else**
34:     **for** $i = 1 \, to \, v$ **do**
35:         **if** $Hungarian(i, 1) == 0$ **then**
36:             $Role_1 \leftarrow i$
37:         **else**
38:             **if** $Hungarian(i, 2) == 0$ **then**
39:                 $Role_2 \leftarrow i$
40:             **else**
41:                 $Role_3 \leftarrow i$
42:             **end if**
43:         **end if**
44:     **end for**
45: **end if**

---

communication along with communicating with the backbone pertinent to its group's status. This is primarily done in order to alleviate the excessive network management overhead [11, 29, 32, 33].

The notion of clustering has been studied over the years and subsequently implemented in mobile ad hoc networks [34]. However, owing to a highly scalable and dynamic topology of IoV networks along with its several other unique characteristics, the conventional clustering techniques in fact do not translate very well for the vehicular networking environments. Furthermore, considering the significance of a cluster head's role within a cluster, a dishonest vehicle if elected as a cluster head, would have dire repercussions. Therefore, selection of an optimal vehicle for the role of a cluster head is undoubtedly of paramount importance. Also, possessing the highest trust score does not necessarily entitle any vehicle to exercise the role of a cluster head. Instead, in addition to being labeled as trustworthy, a vehicle which can guarantee the efficacy of the entire cluster befits the role of a cluster head.

Therefore, three roles, i.e., a cluster head, a proxy cluster head, and members (followers), are introduced and vehicles befitting these roles are, therefore, selected for every cluster via employing the Hungarian algorithm (see Algorithm 2) which ensures an optimal assignment of roles among the entities of a cluster. It is pertinent to mention that the elections would be only triggered if the existing roles' assignment no longer guarantees the efficacy of the cluster, i.e., both the cluster head, and its alternative, the proxy cluster head, are in fact unable to guarantee the overall cluster's efficacy.

For every election, a matrix is generated encompassing the Hungarian cost metric values of vehicles, at that respective time instance, delineated in rows with their corresponding roles in columns (as depicted in Equation 4.6). Since three roles have to be assigned to the vehicles in a cluster, three test scenarios were accordingly constituted, wherein the Hungarian cost metric of each vehicle was computed.

$$
HungarianCostMatrix = \begin{array}{c} \\ v_1 \\ v_2 \\ \vdots \\ v_N \end{array} \overset{\displaystyle Role_1 \quad Role_2 \quad \ldots \quad Role_p}{\left[\begin{array}{cccc} a_{11} & a_{12} & \cdots & a_{1p} \\ a_{21} & a_{22} & \cdots & a_{2p} \\ \vdots & \vdots & \ddots & \vdots \\ a_{N1} & a_{N2} & \cdots & a_{Np} \end{array} \right]} \quad (4.6)
$$

The optimal role assignment via employing Hungarian algorithm is ascertained as:

$$
E = max_b \, Z(b) = maximize \sum_{i=1}^{N} \sum_{r=1}^{p} b_{ir} \, a_{ir} \quad (4.7)
$$

The function Z signifies the overall efficacy of a vehicular cluster. E herein denotes the optimal role of a vehicle amongst all the possible role assignments for achieving the most optimized role assignment, p is the number of roles, a_{ir}

represents the composite metric value of a vehicle i in role r, and $b_{ir} = \{0, 1\}$ subject to:

$$\sum_{i=1}^{N} b_{ir} = 1, \; r = 1, ..., p \; \& \; \sum_{r=1}^{p} b_{ir} \leq 1, \; i = 1, ..., N \qquad (4.8)$$

Equation 4.8 here ensures that only one vehicle can be elected for each role and that no more than one role is allocated to each of the vehicle. The remaining vehicles in a vehicular cluster automatically assume the role of a follower. A vehicle i is assigned to a role r only if the corresponding b_{ir} equals to *1*.

Furthermore, the direction (Eq. 4.9), position (Eq. 4.10), and the mobility (Eq. 4.11) of vehicles have been taken into consideration to segregate them into two clusters [35].

$$\theta_{i,j} = cos^{-1} \frac{i_x j_x + i_y j_y}{\sqrt{i_x^2 + i_y^2}\sqrt{j_x^2 + j_y^2}} \qquad (4.9)$$

herein, i_x, i_y, j_x, and j_y are the xth and y^{th} elements of the normalized vector of vehicles i and j, respectively. Two vehicles, i and j, move in a similar direction if $0 \leq \theta < 45$.

$$Pos_{i,j} = \sqrt{(X_i - X_j)^2 + (Y_i - Y_j)^2} \qquad (4.10)$$

wherein, (X_i, Y_i) and (X_j, Y_j) represent the locations of vehicle i and j, respectively.

$$Mobility_{i,j} = |V_i - V_j| \qquad (4.11)$$

herein, V_i and V_j represents the velocities of vehicle i and j, respectively.

4.3.4 Adaptive Threshold Computation

Although a static threshold T_{TH} has been introduced in Section 4.3.1 to identify the trusted vehicles and subsequently eradicate the malicious vehicles within a vehicular network, nevertheless, smart malicious vehicles are generally capable of manipulating the entire network since such vehicles not always maintain an adverse behavior but rather dynamically alternate between the malicious and non-malicious behaviors to avoid elimination. Furthermore, such behavioral sessions could smartly vary over time to make the detection of malicious patterns extremely strenuous for both the neighboring vehicles and the localized and centralized network traffic monitoring authorities. Therefore, it is highly indispensable that the smart malicious vehicles are eliminated from a network as soon as they start revealing an adverse sort of a behavior.

One possible solution for addressing such sort of an adverse behavior is to intelligently employ an adaptive threshold detection mechanism as delineated in Algorithm 3. Once the network detects that the trust value of any particular vehicle starts decreasing and is within a certain range of the initial threshold ($T_{TH} < T_{avg_{i,t}} < T_{Inspection}$), it adjusts the corresponding detection threshold for that respective vehicle in order to guarantee an early detection of its malicious patterns. In this manner, while a malicious vehicle is busy pursuing the malicious activities in its attacking time window, it could be identified and accordingly eliminated from the network. Therefore, whenever the trust value of a particular vehicle at any time instance is lower in contrast to that of its preceding time instance, and provided that it falls within a certain range of the initial threshold, then the threshold is increased by a factor β equivalent to the difference of both the trust values, i.e., a vehicle's trust value at the preceding time instance and the current time instance. Equation 4.12 here represents the mathematical relation for the envisaged adaptive threshold mechanism:

$$AdaptiveThreshold = \begin{cases} 0.5 + \beta, & \text{if } \beta > 0. \\ 0.5, & \text{otherwise.} \end{cases} \tag{4.12}$$

This suggests that regardless of the value of the initial threshold, the envisaged adaptive threshold mechanism is capable of detecting the smart malicious vehicles earlier as compared to the static threshold mechanism. Furthermore, the higher the initial threshold is, the earlier is the detection of the malicious vehicles (see, Equation 4.13).

$$Detection\ Time_{MaliciousVehicle} \propto \frac{1}{Initial\ Threshold} \tag{4.13}$$

Nevertheless, an honest vehicle may experience a considerable level of decay in its trust score provided that its participation remains low in an IoV network primarily in a bid to safeguard its depleting resources and could be ultimately eliminated via such an adaptive threshold mechanism. Hence, an appropriate inspection time ($t_{inspection}$) needs to be further put into place, wherein once a particular vehicle gets marked via the adaptive threshold, the respective local authority would isolate and accordingly inspect the behavior of such a vehicle for a certain duration of time. After the due inspection period, if the behavior of the said vehicle has not improved to a considerable extent, then that vehicle should be ultimately eliminated out of an IoV network.

4.4 Experimental Results and Performance Analysis

Simulations of the envisaged system model have been carried out via Java and MATLAB with the former one employed for designing an IoV-based simulator, whereas, the later one for carefully analyzing the simulation results. The simulation time has been set to approximately 10 minutes and the simulation area encompasses vehicles traversing in a road network with randomized

---

Algorithm 3 Adaptive threshold computation

1: **for** $t = 2\, to\, T$ **do**
2:   **for** $i = 1\, to\, n$ **do**
3:     $T_{TH} \leftarrow Initial\_Threshold$
4:   **end for**
5:   **if** $Tavg_{i,t} < Tavg_{i,t-1}$ **then**
6:     $\beta \leftarrow Diff(Tavg_{i,t-1}, Tavg_{i,t})$
7:     $T_{TH_{i,t}} \leftarrow T_{TH_{i,t}} + \beta$
8:   **else**
9:     **if** $Tavg_{i,t} \geq Tavg_{i,t-1}$ **then**
10:       $T_{TH_{i,t}} \leftarrow T_{TH}$
11:     **end if**
12:   **end if**
13:   **if** $Tavg_{i,t} < T_{TH_{i,t}}$ **then**
14:     $Veh_{mal} \leftarrow veh_i$
15:   **end if**
16: **end for**

---

speeds, which over time, segregate into two clusters by primarily taking into consideration their respective traveling direction, position, and the mobility. Hence, vehicles within their respective clusters communicate, i.e., interact, with the other vehicles and exchange messages in the process of the same. It is pertinent to mention that vehicles in an IoV network interact with the other vehicles for realizing a number of safety and non-safety, i.e., infotainment, applications and services. Since direct trust is a vehicle's direct observation about the targeted vehicle, we have ascertained the same in terms of the proportion of the number of successful interactions to the total number of interactions between a trustor and a trustee. Furthermore, smart malicious vehicles have been injected within an IoV network which possess the capability of launching an on-off attack, i.e., they dynamically alter between an honest and a dishonest behavior in a bid to avoid being classified as a menace and subsequently getting disposed from the network. In simpler words, they pretend to be cooperative at some of the time instances, whereas, exhibit an adverse behavior on the other with an intent to manipulate the IoV network for malicious gains. In order to simulate such sort of an on-off attack, a purely randomized strategy has been employed so as to ensure a realistic attack scenario since smart malicious vehicles (a) might act cooperative for a certain duration of time before instigating a non-cooperative behavior, (b) manifest a cooperative and a non-cooperative behavior to a varying degree, i.e., could be either less or more cooperative and non-cooperative in terms of their behavior, and (c) demonstrate a non-probabilistic nature in a bid to ensure that a behavioral pattern does not become apparent which could result in their easy detection via the misbehavior identification systems. Such a randomized strategy has been hence realized via the *random()* method (function) in Java which gets invoked each time a smart malicious vehicle comes in an interaction with the other vehicles in an IoV network, thereby enabling it to act in a cooperative (honest) or a non-cooperative (dishonest) mode.

For visualization purposes, trust scores pertinent to only 11 vehicles have been portrayed in Figure 4.1. Furthermore, the minimum acceptable threshold, T_{TH}, has been set to *0.5* and the same could be adjusted in respect of both the network's condition and the vehicles' behavior over time. The elimination of the malicious vehicles, i.e., the ones possessing trust scores beneath the minimum acceptable threshold, could also be observed at time instances $t = 28^{th}$ and $t = 54^{th}$. For the sake of the readers' convenience and to facilitate visuality, the trust scores of each of these vehicles is presented in an individualized manner in Figure 4.2.

Figure 4.3 further depicts the performance of two vehicular clusters in terms of their composite metric values in a particular time window. The said window for both of these clusters has been selected in order to illustrate the impact of the elections and/or any subsequent changes on each of these clusters over the time. Vehicles are segregated into clusters in accordance with their traveling direction, relative velocity, and position and this particular information could be ascertained by all the vehicles from their GPS [35]. Furthermore, the matrices presented in both Table 4.1 and Table 4.2 delineate the Hungarian cost metric values of the vehicles in these clusters, i.e., in cluster A and cluster B, at the random time instances within the selected time window. R_1 here characterizes the role of a cluster head, whereas, R_2 and R_3 represent the roles of a proxy cluster head and the follower(s), respectively. The shaded entries (within these tables) demonstrate the optimal role assignment of the vehicles for their corresponding cluster. As quite apparent from both of Table 4.1 and Table 4.2, the roles assigned via the Hungarian algorithm are optimum and, therefore, result in enhancing the resource efficacy of the clusters. Also, in Table 4.1, vehicle 1, and in Table 4.2, vehicles 3, 5, and 6 have not been allocated any roles, and thus, they automatically assume role of a follower.

It is pertinent to note that the cluster head for cluster A remains consistent all through, whereas, the cluster head for cluster B changes at time instances $t = 51^{st}$ and $t = 53^{rd}$ since they could no longer guarantee the optimal resource efficacy of the overall cluster. Moreover, Figure 4.4 portrays the stability of both of these clusters primarily in terms of selection of a

TABLE 4.1

Hungarian cost metric – Cluster A ($t = 29^{th}$)

$v \backslash R$	R_1	R_2	R_3
v_1	0.450329621	0.447041476	0.075038819
v_2	0.395421458	0.749966033	0.303205767
v_3	0.741470699	0.262690672	0.036464067
v_4	0.337002756	0.222211928	0.147200619

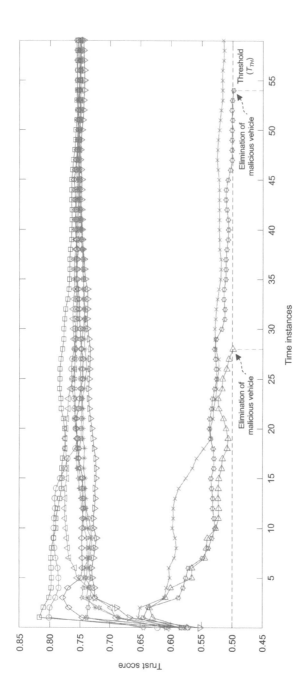

FIGURE 4.1
Depicting the trust scores of 11 random vehicles over the simulated time duration (each of the time instance corresponds to 10 seconds). The malicious vehicles have been eliminated at the time instances $t = 28^{th}$ and $t = 54^{th}$. It could be further observed that the trustworthy vehicles largely tend to achieve a more stable trust score since they continuously act in a reliable manner over time, whereas, a considerable decay is observable within the trust scores of the malicious vehicles primarily owing to their untrustworthy nature.

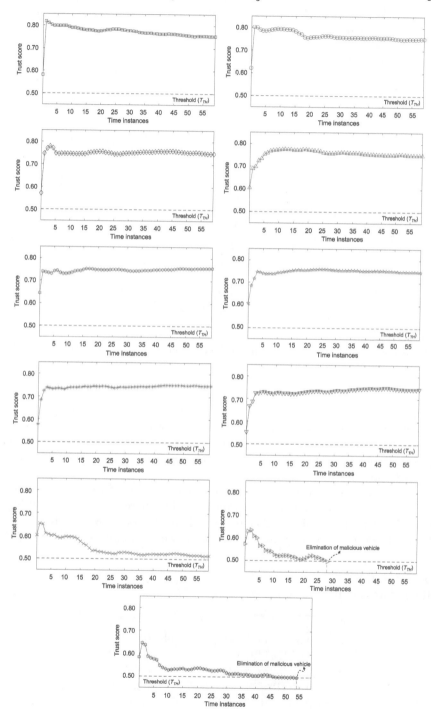

FIGURE 4.2

Depicting the trust scores of vehicles in an individualized manner over the simulated time duration.

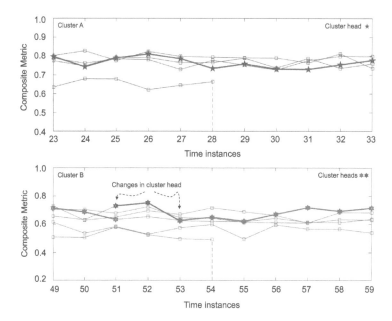

FIGURE 4.3
Depicting the optimal cluster head (and their followers) for the respective clusters.

secure and resource efficient cluster head via our Hungarian-based optimal role assignment scheme and that proved to be considerably stable in comparison to the conventional cluster head selection mechanisms, i.e., the ones which primarily opt for a vehicle with the highest trust score in a vehicular cluster as its cluster head.

Figure 4.5, on the contrary, delineates on the notion of an adaptive threshold as already illustrated in the section 4.3.4. Therefore, as a malicious vehicle starts revealing its smart malicious behaviour, its corresponding trust score begins to decline, thereby prompting the network to induce a factor of β in

TABLE 4.2
Hungarian cost metric – Cluster B $(t = 51^{st})$

$v \backslash R$	R_1	R_2	R_3
v_1	0.095274501	0.607088244	0.443397002
v_2	0.564751491	0.182397733	0.593022174
v_3	0.302523288	0.174730398	0.402930397
v_4	0.408489671	0.43277038	0.206001369
v_5	0.287871657	0.277055971	0.119456181
v_6	0.039171268	0.212836268	0.253762851

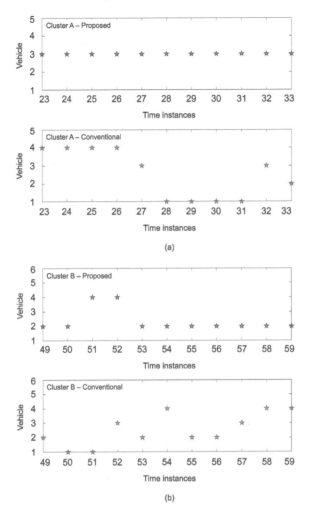

FIGURE 4.4
Clusters A and B's stability via our envisaged Hungarian-based optimal role assignment scheme vis-á-vis other conventional cluster head selection mechanisms, i.e., the ones which opt for a vehicle with the highest trust score within a vehicular cluster as its cluster head.

its respective detection threshold, i.e., the factor β is generally equivalent to the difference of the trust scores of a malicious vehicle at the preceding time instance and at the current time instance. It is quite apparent that it took a much longer time to detect a malicious vehicle with static threshold as shown in Figure 4.5(a) in contrast to the adaptive threshold as depicted in Figure 4.5(b), i.e., the vehicles that were detected as malicious ones at time instances $t = 28^{th}$ and $t = 54^{th}$ with static threshold were detected as malicious at time instances $t = 11^{th}$ and $t = 28^{th}$ via the adaptive threshold.

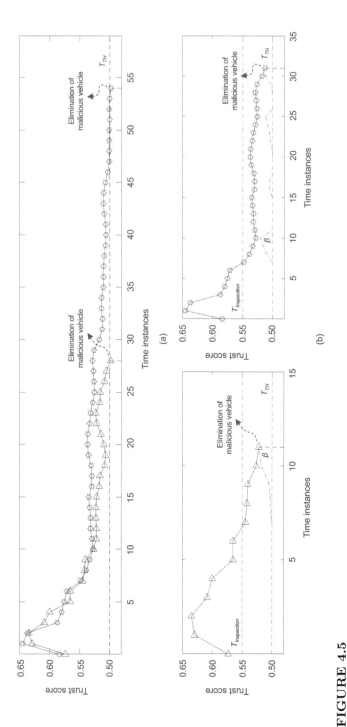

FIGURE 4.5
Depicting the elimination of malicious vehicles via (a) static threshold and (b) adaptive threshold over the simulated time duration, i.e., the malicious vehicles in the case of a static threshold have been eliminated at time instances $t = 28^{th}$ and $t = 54^{th}$, whereas, at time instances $t = 11^{th}$ and $t = 28^{th}$ in the case of an adaptive threshold.

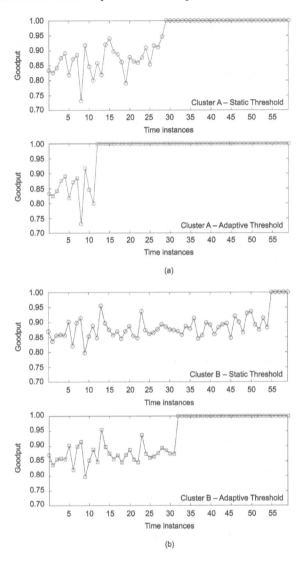

FIGURE 4.6

Depicting the goodput of Clusters A and B via (a) static threshold and (b) adaptive threshold.

Figure 4.6 depicts the goodput $(0 \leq G \leq 1)$, i.e., the ratio of the legitimate packets received to the total number of packets successfully received by vehicles within a given IoV cluster, i.e., at each time instance. In order to ascertain the same, the number of packets disseminated by the honest vehicles are considered as the legitimate ones, whereas, packets disseminated by the malicious vehicles are flagged as the counterfeited ones. It could be hence observed from Figure 4.6 that in the case of an adaptive threshold, the good-put of the network approached to its maximum, i.e., at *1*, earlier in contrast to the static threshold since counterfeited packets have been eliminated fairly earlier from an IoV network.

4.5 Summary

An intelligent transportation system is considered as one of the most indispensable constituents within the context of the smart cities in a bid to realize highly safe and efficacious traffic flows. It facilitates vehicles to communicate with the other road entities and the supporting infrastructure via vehicle-to-everything communication to guarantee both safety-critical and non-safety (infotainment) applications. Nevertheless, road entities in such sort of an IoV network are also prone to a number of internal and external attacks with the former one unable to be identified via the classical security, i.e., cryptographic-based, schemes. In this chapter, we have envisaged a scalable hybrid trust model which is capable of ensuring both the real-time identification and eradication of multiple malicious vehicles via employing a composite metric (encompassing the weighted amalgamation of a vehicle's computed trust score and its corresponding available resources) in order to guarantee that the stringent performance requirements of the safety-critical vehicular applications could be entirely met. A Hungarian algorithm based optimal role assignment scheme has been further envisaged for selecting an optimal cluster head, proxy cluster head, and followers among the members of a vehicular cluster for maximizing its overall efficacy. Furthermore, the notion of an adaptive threshold has been put forward for identifying and subsequently eliminating the smart malicious vehicles from the network in a timely manner, i.e., as soon as they start exhibiting an adverse behavior, to ensure that the network could not be manipulated for any sort of malicious gains. In the near future, the authors intend to extend this research work via addressing the notion of selfish vehicles, i.e., the ones which only participate in the network when it best suits their own interest, to incentivize their persistent participation for enhancing the overall network performance.

Bibliography

[1] Aljawharah Alnasser, Hongjian Sun, and Jing Jiang. Recommendation-Based Trust Model for Vehicle-to-Everything (V2X). *IEEE Internet of Things Journal*, 7(1):440–450, 2020.

[2] Farhan Ahmad, Virginia N. L. Franqueira, and Asma Adnane. TEAM: A Trust Evaluation and Management Framework in Context-Enabled Vehicular Ad-Hoc Networks. *IEEE Access*, 6:28643–28660, 2018.

[3] Farhan Ahmad, Fatih Kurugollu, Chaker Abdelaziz Kerrache, Sakir Sezer, and Lu Liu. NOTRINO: A Novel Hybrid Trust Management Scheme for Internet-of-Vehicles. *IEEE Transactions on Vehicular Technology*, 70(9):9244–9257, 2021.

[4] Rasheed Hussain, Jooyoung Lee, and Sherali Zeadally. Trust in VANET: A Survey of Current Solutions and Future Research Opportunities. *IEEE Transactions on Intelligent Transportation Systems*, 22(5):2553–2571, 2021.

[5] Barry Sheehan, Finbarr Murphy, Martin Mullins, and Cian Ryan. Connected and Autonomous Vehicles: A Cyber-risk Classification Framework. *Transportation Research – Part A: Policy and Practice*, 124:523–536, 2019.

[6] Surbhi Sharma and Baijnath Kaushik. A Survey on Internet of Vehicles: Applications, Security Issues & Solutions. *Vehicular Communications*, 20:100182, 2019.

[7] Moayad Aloqaily, Safa Otoum, Ismaeel Al Ridhawi, and Yaser Jararweh. An Intrusion Detection System for Connected Vehicles in Smart Cities. *Ad Hoc Networks*, 90:101842, 2019.

[8] Kamran Ahmad Awan, Ikram Ud Din, Ahmad Almogren, Mohsen Guizani, and Sonia Khan. StabTrust — A Stable and Centralized Trust-Based Clustering Mechanism for IoT Enabled Vehicular Ad-Hoc Networks. *IEEE Access*, 8:21159–21177, 2020.

[9] Amira Kchaou, Ryma Abassi, and Sihem Guemara. Towards the Performance Evaluation of a Clustering and Trust Based Security Mechanism for VANET. In *Proceedings of the 15th International Conference on Availability, Reliability and Security*, ARES'20, New York, NY, USA, 2020. Association for Computing Machinery.

[10] Amira Kchaou, Ryma Abassi, and Sihem Guemara El Fatmi. Towards a Secured Clustering Mechanism for Messages Exchange in VANET. In *2018 32nd International Conference on Advanced Information Networking and Applications Workshops (WAINA)*, pages 88–93, 2018.

[11] Sarah Oubabas, Rachida Aoudjit, Joel J. P. C. Rodrigues, and Said Talbi. Secure and Stable Vehicular Ad Hoc Network Clustering Algorithm based on Hybrid Mobility Similarities and Trust Management Scheme. *Vehicular Communications*, 13:128–138, 2018.

[12] Ryma Abassi, Aida Ben Chehida Douss, and Damien Sauveron. TSME: A Trust-based Security Scheme for Message Exchange in Vehicular Ad hoc Networks. *Human-centric Computing and Information Sciences*, 10(1):43, 2020.

[13] R. Sugumar, A. Rengarajan, and C. Jayakumar. Trust Based Authentication Technique for Cluster Based Vehicular Ad Hoc Networks (VANET). *Wireless Networks*, 24(2):373–382, 2018.

[14] Muhammad Sameer Sheikh, Jun Liang, and Wensong Wang. A Survey of Security Services, Attacks, and Applications for Vehicular Ad Hoc Networks (VANETs). *Sensors*, 19(16):3589, 2019.

[15] Ibrahim Abdo Rai, Riaz Ahmed Shaikh, and Syed Raheel Hassan. A Hybrid Dual-mode Trust Management Scheme for Vehicular Networks. *International Journal of Distributed Sensor Networks*, 16(7), 2020.

[16] Adnan Mahmood, Bernard Butler, Wei Emma Zhang, Quan Z. Sheng, and Sarah Ali Siddiqui. A Hybrid Trust Management Heuristic for VANETs. In *2019 IEEE International Conference on Pervasive Computing and Communications Workshops (PerCom Workshops)*, pages 748–752, 2019.

[17] Ghani-Ur Rehman, Anwar Ghani, Muhammad Zubair, Syed Husnain A. Naqvi, Dhananjay Singh, and Shad Muhammad. IPS: Incentive and Punishment Scheme for Omitting Selfishness in the Internet of Vehicles (Iov). *IEEE Access*, 7:109026–109037, 2019.

[18] Ghani-Ur Rehman, Anwar Ghani, Shad Muhammad, Madhusudan Singh, and Dhananjay Singh. Selfishness in Vehicular Delay-Tolerant Networks: A Review. *Sensors*, 20(10):3000, 2020.

[19] Adnan Mahmood, Sarah Ali Siddiqui, Quan Z. Sheng, Wei Emma Zhang, Hajime Suzuki, and Wei Ni. Trust on Wheels: Towards Secure and Resource Efficient IoV Networks. *Computing*, 104(6):1337–1358, 2022.

[20] Palak Bagga, Ashok Kumar Das, Mohammad Wazid, Joel J. P. C. Rodrigues, and Youngho Park. Authentication Protocols in Internet of Vehicles: Taxonomy, Analysis, and Challenges. *IEEE Access*, 8:54314–54344, 2020.

[21] Chaker Abdelaziz Kerrache, Carlos T. Calafate, Juan-Carlos Cano, Nasreddine Lagraa, and Pietro Manzoni. Trust Management for Vehicular Networks: An Adversary-Oriented Overview. *IEEE Access*, 4:9293–9307, 2016.

[22] Muhammad Baqer Mollah, Jun Zhao, Dusit Niyato, Yong Liang Guan, Chau Yuen, Sumei Sun, Kwok-Yan Lam, and Leong Hai Koh. Blockchain for the Internet of Vehicles Towards Intelligent Transportation Systems: A Survey. *IEEE Internet of Things Journal*, 8(6):4157–4185, 2021.

[23] Vishal Sharma. An Energy-Efficient Transaction Model for the Blockchain-Enabled Internet of Vehicles (IoV). *IEEE Communications Letters*, 23(2):246–249, 2019.

[24] Chao Wang, Xiaoman Cheng, Jitong Li, Yunhua He, and Ke Xiao. A Survey: Applications of Blockchain in the Internet of Vehicles. *EURASIP Journal on Wireless Communications and Networking*, 2021(1):77, Apr 2021.

[25] Sarah Ali Siddiqui, Adnan Mahmood, Quan Z. Sheng, Hajime Suzuki, and Wei Ni. A Survey of Trust Management in the Internet of Vehicles. *Electronics*, 10(18):2223, 2021.

[26] Farhan Ahmad, Asma Adnane, Chaker A. Kerrache, Fatih Kurugollu, and Iain Phillips. On the Design, Development and Implementation of Trust Evaluation Mechanism in Vehicular Networks. In *2019 IEEE/ACS 16th International Conference on Computer Systems and Applications (AICCSA)*, pages 1–7, 2019.

[27] Jinsong Zhang, Kangfeng Zheng, Dongmei Zhang, and Bo Yan. AATMS: An Anti-Attack Trust Management Scheme in VANET. *IEEE Access*, 8:21077–21090, 2020.

[28] Ji-Ming Chen, Ting-Ting Li, and John Panneerselvam. TMEC: A Trust Management Based on Evidence Combination on Attack-Resistant and Collaborative Internet of Vehicles. *IEEE Access*, 7:148913–148922, 2019.

[29] Hamssa Hasrouny, Abed Ellatif Samhat, Carole Bassil, and Anis Laouiti. Trust Model for Secure Group Leader-based Communications in VANET. *Wireless Networks*, 25(8):4639–4661, Nov 2019.

[30] Xumin Huang, Rong Yu, Jiawen Kang, and Yan Zhang. Distributed Reputation Management for Secure and Efficient Vehicular Edge Computing and Networks. *IEEE Access*, 5:25408–25420, 2017.

[31] Yining Liu, Keqiu Li, Yingwei Jin, Yong Zhang, and Wenyu Qu. A Novel Reputation Computation Model Based on Subjective Logic for Mobile Ad hoc Networks. *Future Generation Computer Systems*, 27(5):547–554, 2011.

[32] Kashif Naseer Qureshi, Muhammad Moghees Idrees, Jaime Lloret, and Ignacio Bosch. Self-Assessment Based Clustering Data Dissemination for Sparse and Dense Traffic Conditions for Internet of Vehicles. *IEEE Access*, 8:10363–10372, 2020.

[33] Ashit Kumar Dutta, Mohamed Elhoseny, Vandna Dahiya, and K. Shankar. An Efficient Hierarchical Clustering Protocol for Multihop Internet of Vehicles Communication. *Transactions on Emerging Telecommunications Technologies*, 31(5):e3690, 2020.

[34] Lin Li, Wenjian Wang, and Zhenhai Gao. Driver's Social Relationship Based Clustering and Transmission in Vehicle Ad Hoc Networks (VANETs). *Electronics*, 9(2):298, 2020.

[35] Yan Huo, Yuejia Liu, Liran Ma, Xiuzhen Cheng, and Tao Jing. An Enhanced Low Overhead and Stable Clustering Scheme for Crossroads in VANETs. *EURASIP Journal on Wireless Communications and Networking*, 2016(1):74, 2016.

5

Conclusion

In this chapter, we summarize the key contributions of this book and delineate the concluding remarks.

The Internet of Vehicles (IoV), as the name suggests, *'vehicles connected to the Internet'*, is an indispensable part of the vehicular communication technologies which can satisfy the stringent performance requirements of the next-generation of fully automated, autonomous, or self-driving vehicles. IoV is typically regarded as an intelligent amalgamation of intervehicular networks, intravehicular networks, and mobile Internet which makes it a large-scale distributed system employed for cooperatively sensing the neighboring environment and for collectively deciding on further maneuvers to undertake. In short, IoV is anticipated to become a key component of the large-scale Internet of Things (IoT) infrastructure and has been receiving a considerable attention from academia and industry recently [1, 2, 3, 4, 5, 6].

Today, vehicles are increasingly leveraging the cloud infrastructure. They are further collecting and transmitting diverse sensory information in a heterogeneous wireless networking environment, i.e., particularly within the dense scenarios, in an attempt to enhance the efficacy of the overall traffic system and safety of the moving vehicles, and especially, of the (vulnerable) pedestrians. Nevertheless, IoV networks are susceptible to both of the internal and external attacks. There are numerous types of attacks that can break the security of an IoV network, including but not limited to, Denial-of-Service (DoS) attack, Distributed DoS (DDoS) attack, jamming, man-in-the-middle attack, malware attack, replay attack, repudiation, Sybil attack, masquerade attack, GPS spoofing, and timing attack [7, 8]. Thus, if a *single* vehicle gets compromised in one way or the other within an IoV network, it can result in jeopardizing the security of the entire networking infrastructure consequently leading to fatal consequences.

Accordingly, this particular book is a humble effort for employing the promising notion of *trust* in a bid to address the security issues of an IoV network primarily since the conventional cryptographic-based techniques are not

DOI: 10.1201/9781003365037-5

optimal for an IoV network owing to its high mobility and highly distributed nature, and vulnerability to a diverse range of internal attacks. Trust is itself a derived quantity and is ascertained for each vehicle in accordance with its behavior, is assessed via the interactions among a trustor and a trustee, and thus, possesses the potential to not only identify but to eliminate any misbehaving vehicle out of the network.

In this regard, Chapter 2 delineated the convergence of the notion of trust with the IoV in terms of not only its underlying rationale but also by highlighting the salient opportunities it offers for strengthening the security of an IoV network along with the challenges which should be intelligently addressed for realizing the deployment of the trusted IoV networks in the context of the smart cities.

Chapter 3 envisaged a distributed trust computational model which accurately ascertained the trust score of a trustee, i.e., a targeted vehicle, by appropriately weighing its trust segments received as a result of a direct interaction of a trustor and a trustee, i.e., direct trust, or obtained as recommendations via the one-hop neighboring vehicles of a trustee, i.e., indirect trust. The weights of these trust segments had been ascertained by taking into consideration the salient features of familiarity, similarity, and timeliness (referred to as the quality attributes). Familiarity facilitated in ascertaining as to how well a one-hop neighbor had been acquainted with that of a targeted vehicle, similarity referred to the degree of similar content (vehicular applications and services and the data involved therein) accessed by a trustor and a trustee, and timeliness delineated the freshness of a reputation segment. An intelligent trust threshold mechanism was further envisaged which identified and evicted misbehaving vehicles from an IoV network in an accurate manner. The introduction of an inspection threshold, along with an allocation of additional time to vehicles being inspected under specific conditions, served as a further check for guaranteeing that only misbehaving vehicles were eliminated from an IoV network and vehicles which were bad-mouthed by the misbehaving vehicles were reintegrated into the network. For purposes of simulation, an IoV simulator had been programmed within Java and the traces accumulated in the form of a data set were subsequently investigated in MATLAB. Experimental results exhibited the strength of the envisaged trust model in terms of optimizing the misbehavior detection and its resilience to attacks.

Chapter 4 envisaged a scalable hybrid trust model, wherein a composite metric (encompassing the weighted amalgamation of a vehicle's computed trust score and its corresponding available resources) had been proposed to guarantee that the stringent performance requirements for the safety-critical vehicular applications can be fully met. It, furthermore, argued on electing a suitable vehicle for the role of a cluster head primarily since connected vehicles in an IoV network are anticipated to organize themselves in the form of the vehicular groups, i.e., clusters, when traversing on the road, and are responsible for the inter-cluster communication, intra-cluster communication, and reporting an entire cluster's status to the backbone network in a bid to alleviate the network management overhead. This can become extremely vulnerable in case a dishonest vehicle ends up ruling the entire cluster since it could yield grave consequences for both the entire network and its users. Nevertheless, possessing of a highest trust score does not necessarily justifies a vehicle's eligibility as a cluster head, since in addition to being trustworthy, a vehicle that can guarantee the overall efficacy of the entire cluster, should be considered as an optimum choice for the role of a cluster head. Accordingly, a Hungarian algorithm-based optimal role assignment scheme had been envisaged for the selection of an optimal cluster head, proxy cluster head, and the followers among the members of a vehicular cluster in order to maximize its overall efficacy. Moreover, the notion of an adaptive threshold had been proposed to identify and subsequently eliminate the smart malicious vehicles from an IoV network in a timely manner, i.e., as soon as they start exhibiting an adverse behavior, to guarantee that the network is not manipulated for any malicious gains. Extensive simulations had been carried out in this regard and performance analysis demonstrated the efficaciousness of our proposed scheme.

A secure and trusted environment is indispensable in the context of the promising yet emerging paradigm of ITS for facilitating the smart vehicles to communicate safety-critical messages with the other vehicles along with the supporting infrastructure. The realization of such an environment is also imperative for the deployment of futuristic smart cities (wherein autonomous vehicles are anticipated to be the main mode of both personal and commercial transportation) and whose success is primarily dependent on factors such as the resiliency of the IoV networks, and the dissemination of authentic and reliable information within the same. It is pertinent to mention that IoV networks are extremely critical in nature since any malicious intruder is capable of jeopardizing the same, and could prove fatal for the vehicular passengers and the vulnerable pedestrians. Therefore, the system (network) designers should opt for complete resilience instead of only introducing the notion of tolerance to malicious behavior within an IoV network. This book, in its entirety, is an effort to strengthen the resilience of the IoV networks via employing the promising notion of trust, and together with an evolution of the state-of-the-art automotive hardware and software, high bandwidth, and low latent communication networks, the envisaged solutions could play an indispensable role in realizing safe and intelligent traffic flows.

Bibliography

[1] Rasheed Hussain, Jooyoung Lee, and Sherali Zeadally. Trust in VANET: A Survey of Current Solutions and Future Research Opportunities. *IEEE Transactions on Intelligent Transportation Systems*, 22(5):2553–2571, 2021.

[2] Yuanzhi Ni, Lin Cai, Jianping He, Alexey Vinel, Yue Li, Hamed Mosavat-Jahromi, and Jianping Pan. Toward Reliable and Scalable Internet of Vehicles: Performance Analysis and Resource Management. *Proceedings of the IEEE*, 108(2):324–340, 2020.

[3] Baofeng Ji, Xueru Zhang, Shahid Mumtaz, Congzheng Han, Chunguo Li, Hong Wen, and Dan Wang. Survey on the Internet of Vehicles: Network Architectures and Applications. *IEEE Communications Standards Magazine*, 4(1):34–41, 2020.

[4] Huimin Lu, Qiang Liu, Daxin Tian, Yujie Li, Hyoungseop Kim, and Seiichi Serikawa. The Cognitive Internet of Vehicles for Autonomous Driving. *IEEE Network*, 33(3):65–73, 2019.

[5] Kai Liu, Xincao Xu, Mengliang Chen, Bingyi Liu, Libing Wu, and Victor C. S. Lee. A Hierarchical Architecture for the Future Internet of Vehicles. *IEEE Communications Magazine*, 57(7):41–47, 2019.

[6] Furqan Jameel, Zheng Chang, Jun Huang, and Tapani Ristaniemi. Internet of Autonomous Vehicles: Architecture, Features, and Socio-Technological Challenges. *IEEE Wireless Communications*, 26(4):21–29, 2019.

[7] Surbhi Sharma and Baijnath Kaushik. A Survey on Internet of Vehicles: Applications, Security Issues & Solutions. *Vehicular Communications*, 20:100182, 2019.

[8] Muhammad Sameer Sheikh, Jun Liang, and Wensong Wang. A Survey of Security Services, Attacks, and Applications for Vehicular Ad Hoc Networks (VANETs). *Sensors*, 19(16):3589, 2019.

Index

Page numbers in **bold** refer to tables and those in *italic* refer to figures.